100 Amazing Patterns
Intricate Designs coloring book
Smita Keisser

This book belongs to

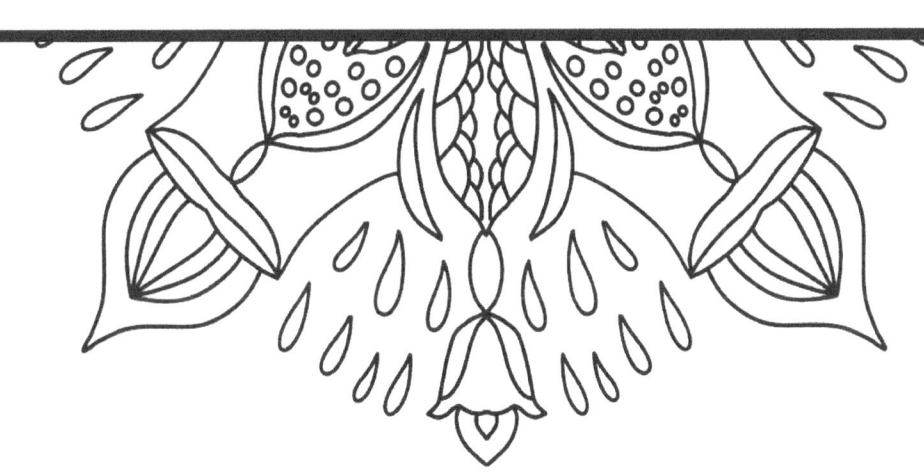

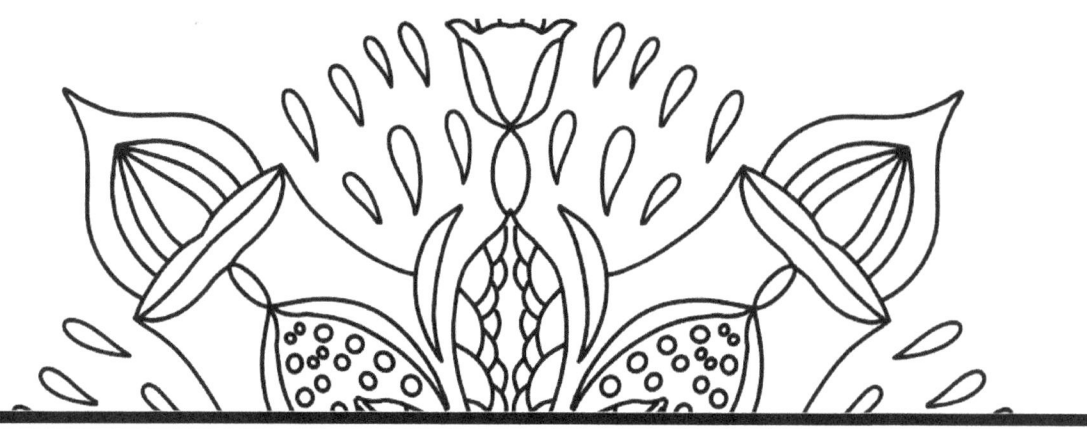

Thank you for your interest in my art designs.
These are my hand drawn designs
some page designs have a name written on the back page
to prompt you to imagine
If you notice some art lines are wonky that's ok.
its my hand shaking when I was drawing
life is not a perfect straight line
we all have bumps, hurdles, mountains that come our way
I hope to inspire you, wash away worries
and
Enjoy Coloring!
Feel free to leave a review

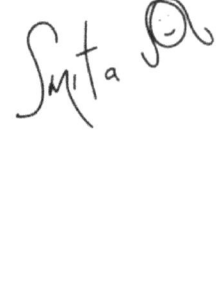

©2022 copyright Smita Keisser All rights reserved
This book may not be reproduced or transmitted in any form or by any means
electronic or mechanical without written permission from the author.

smitakeisser.com

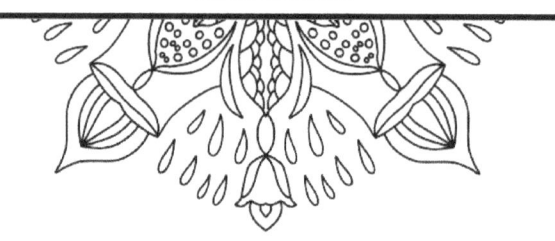

Hope

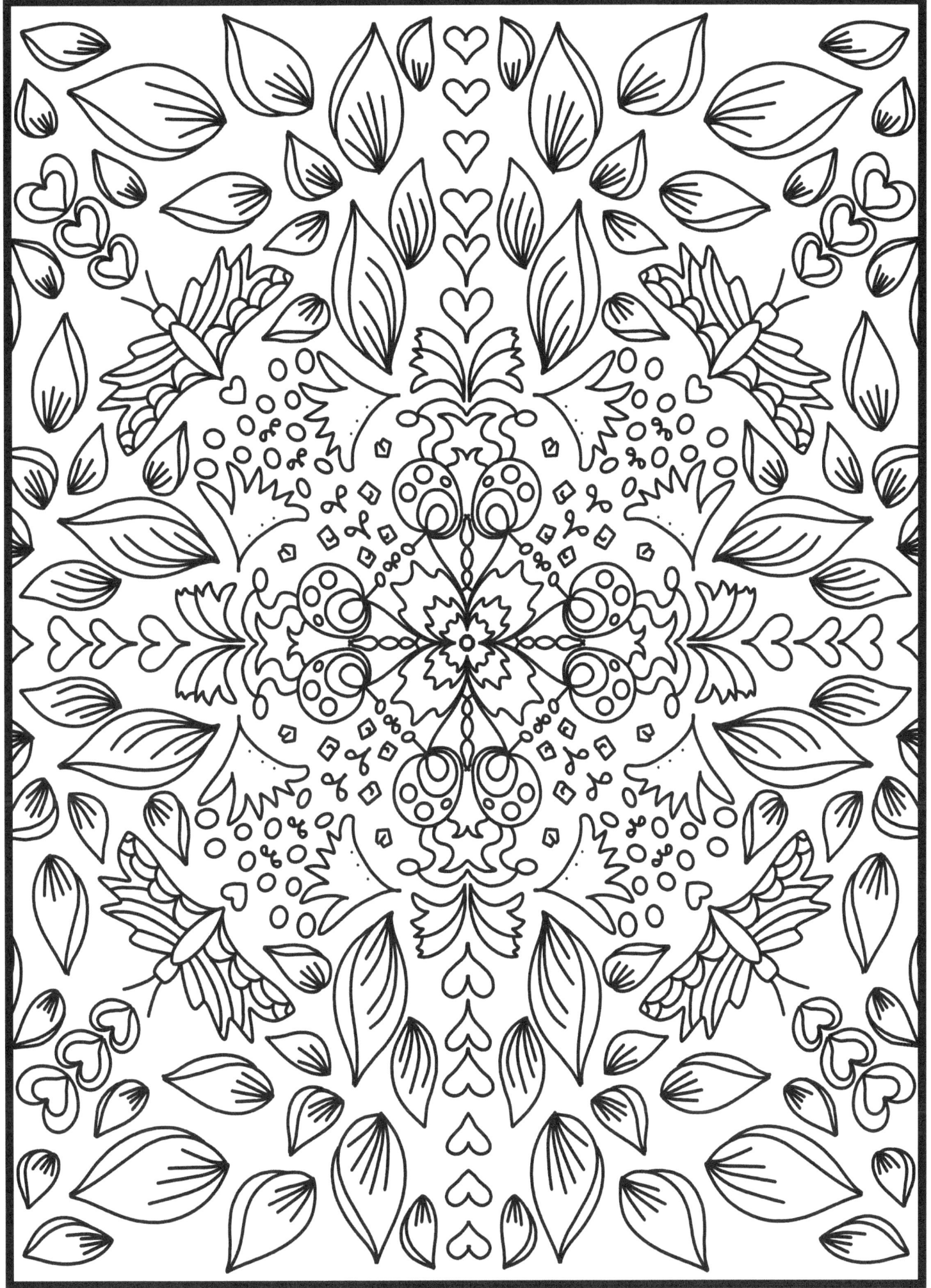

Serene Butterflies

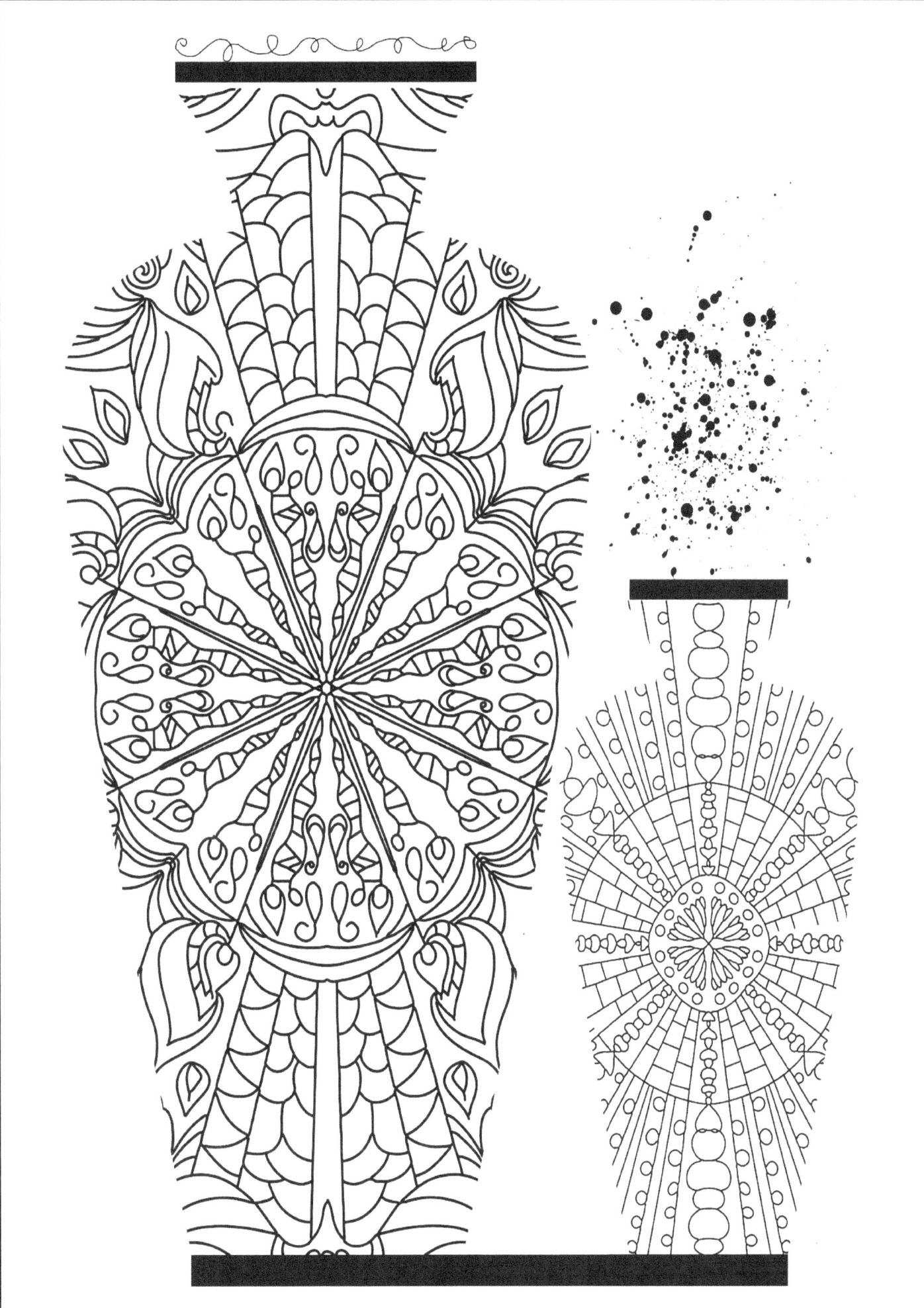

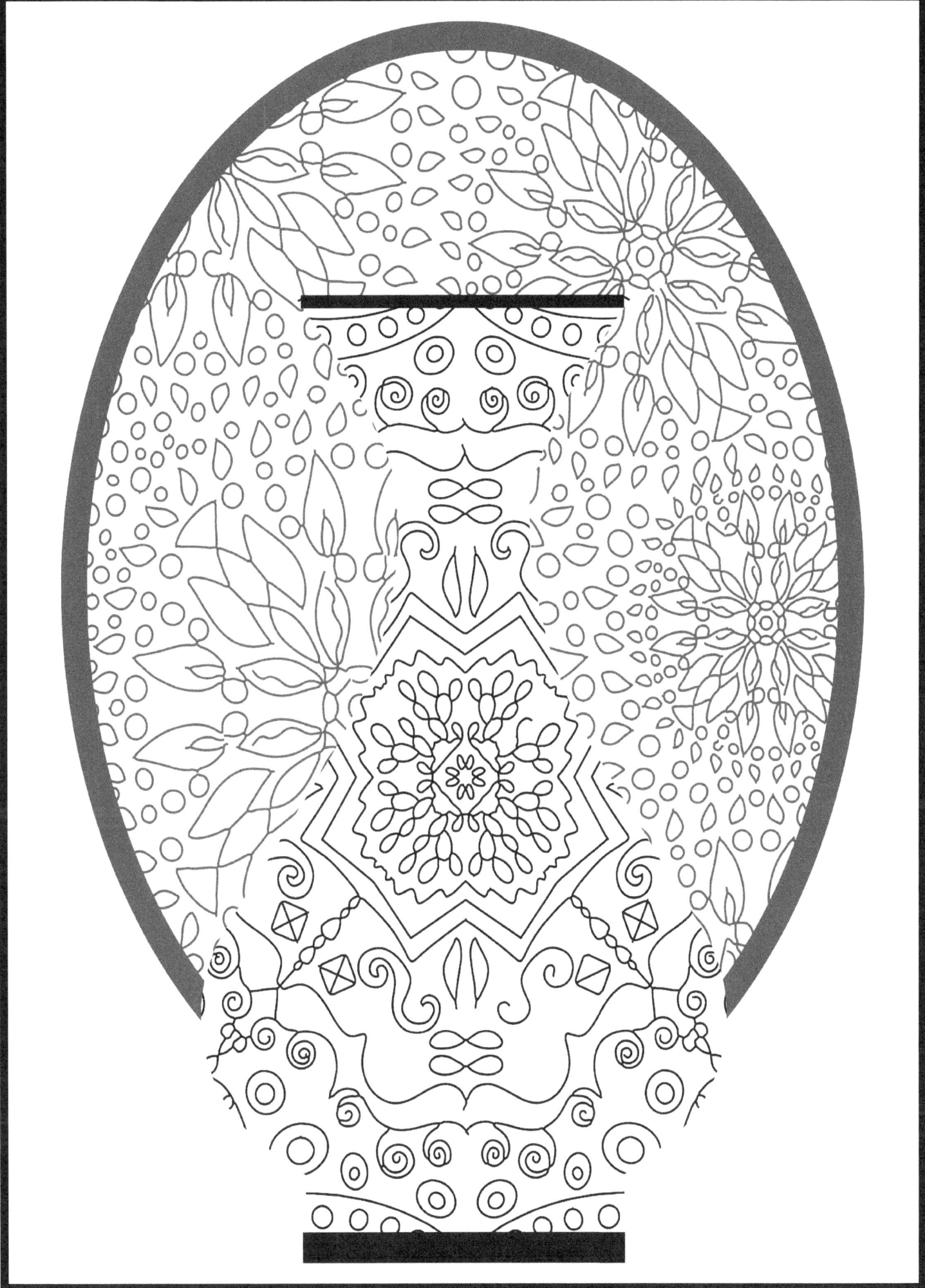

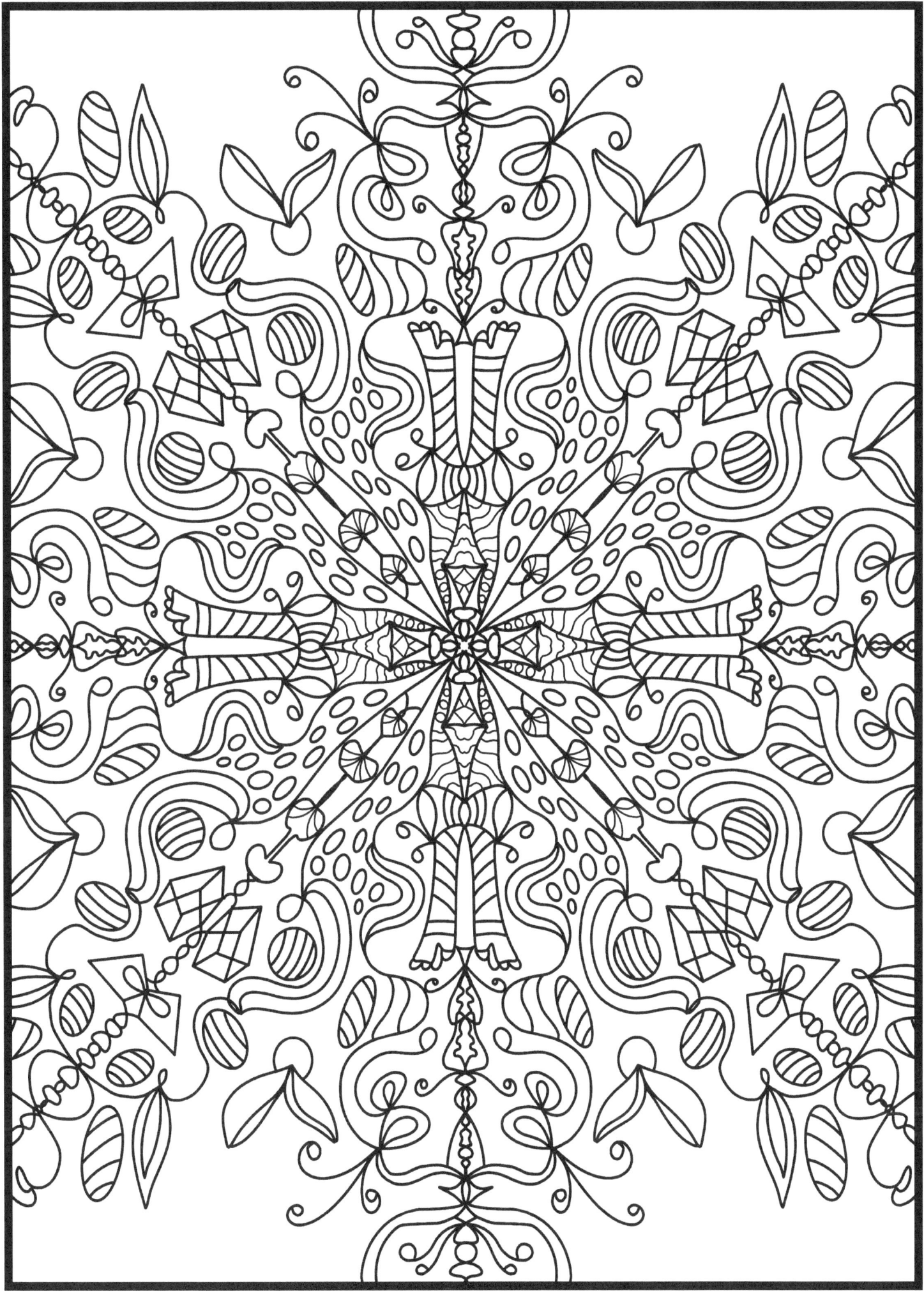

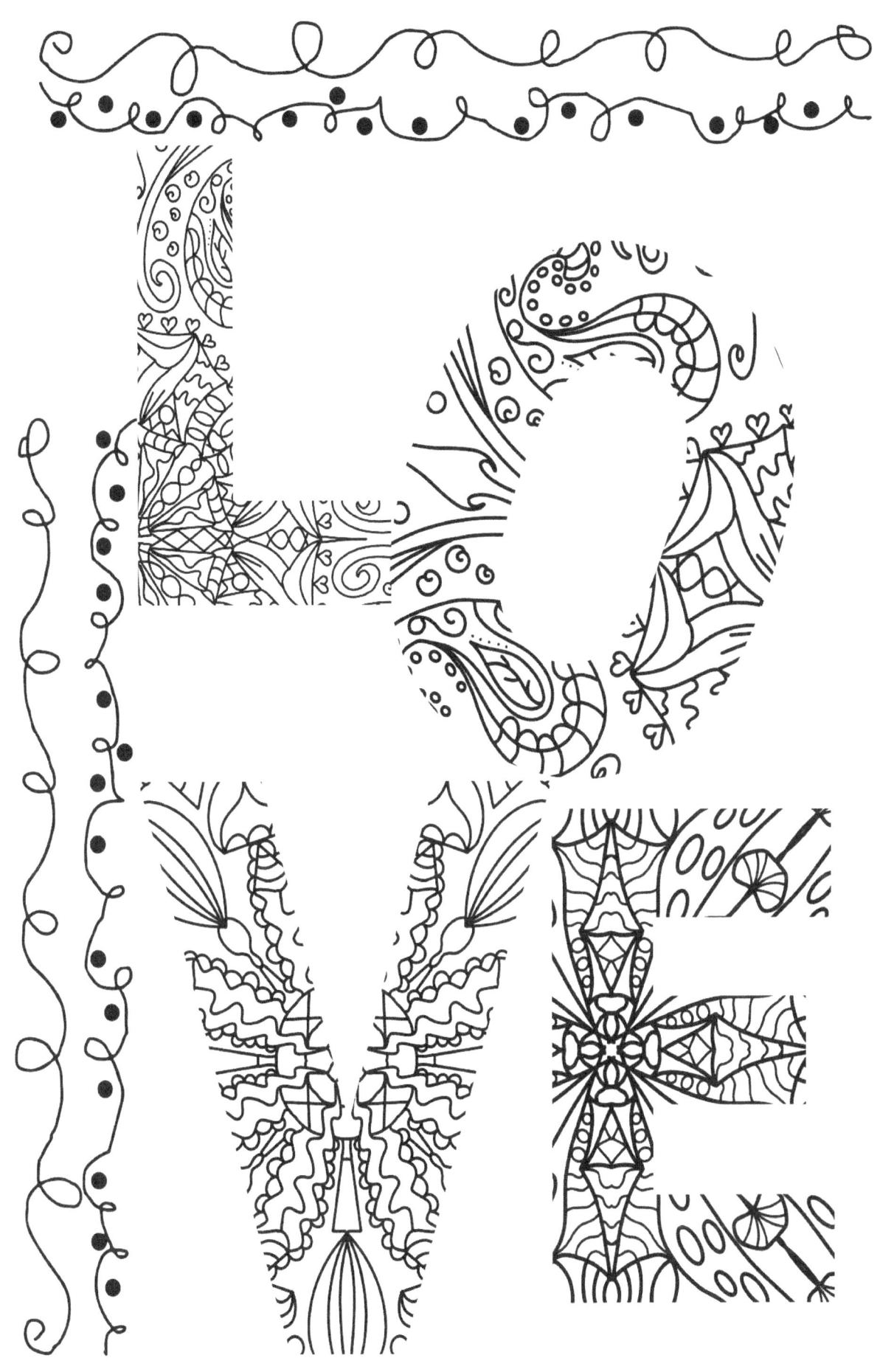

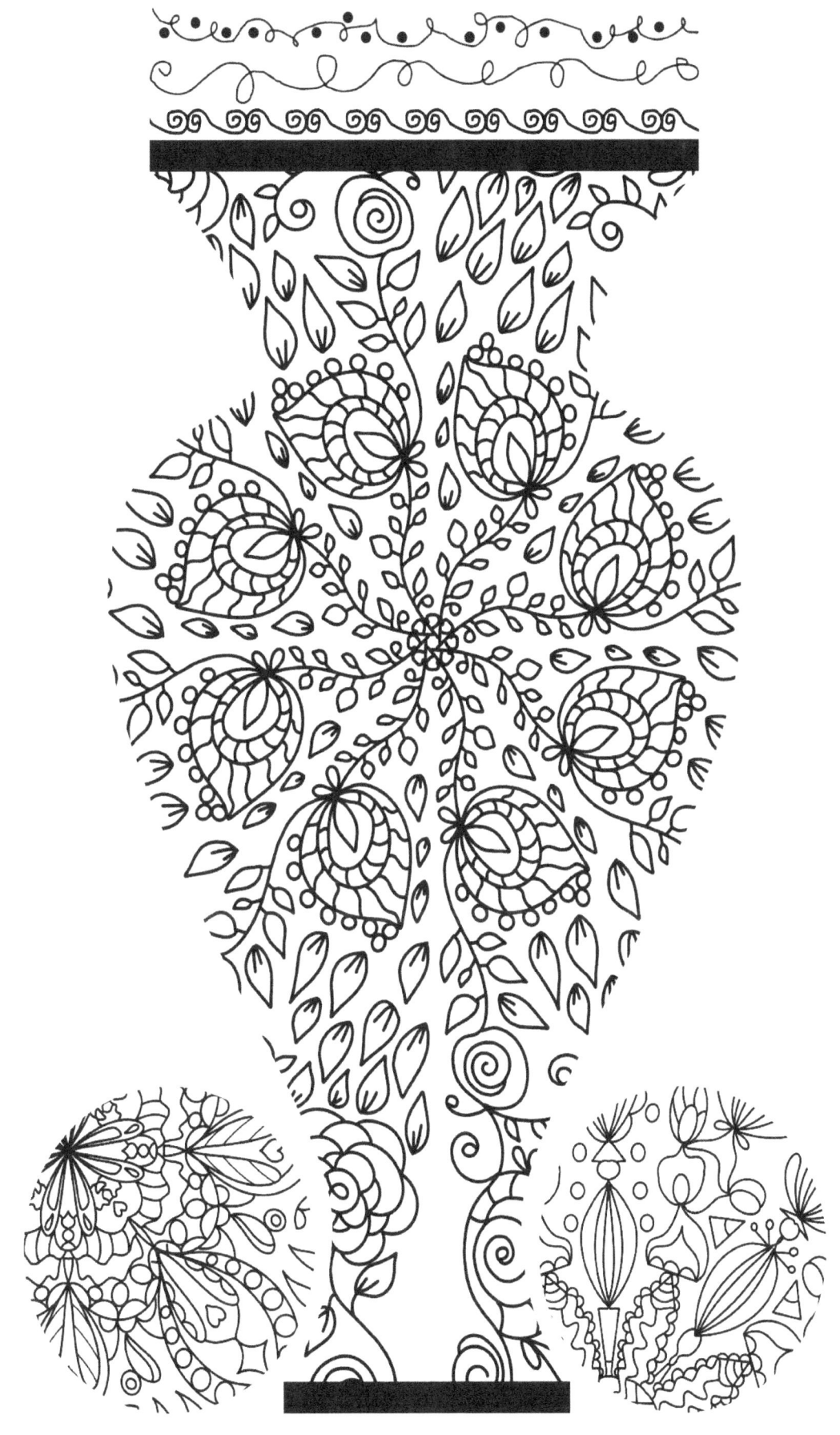

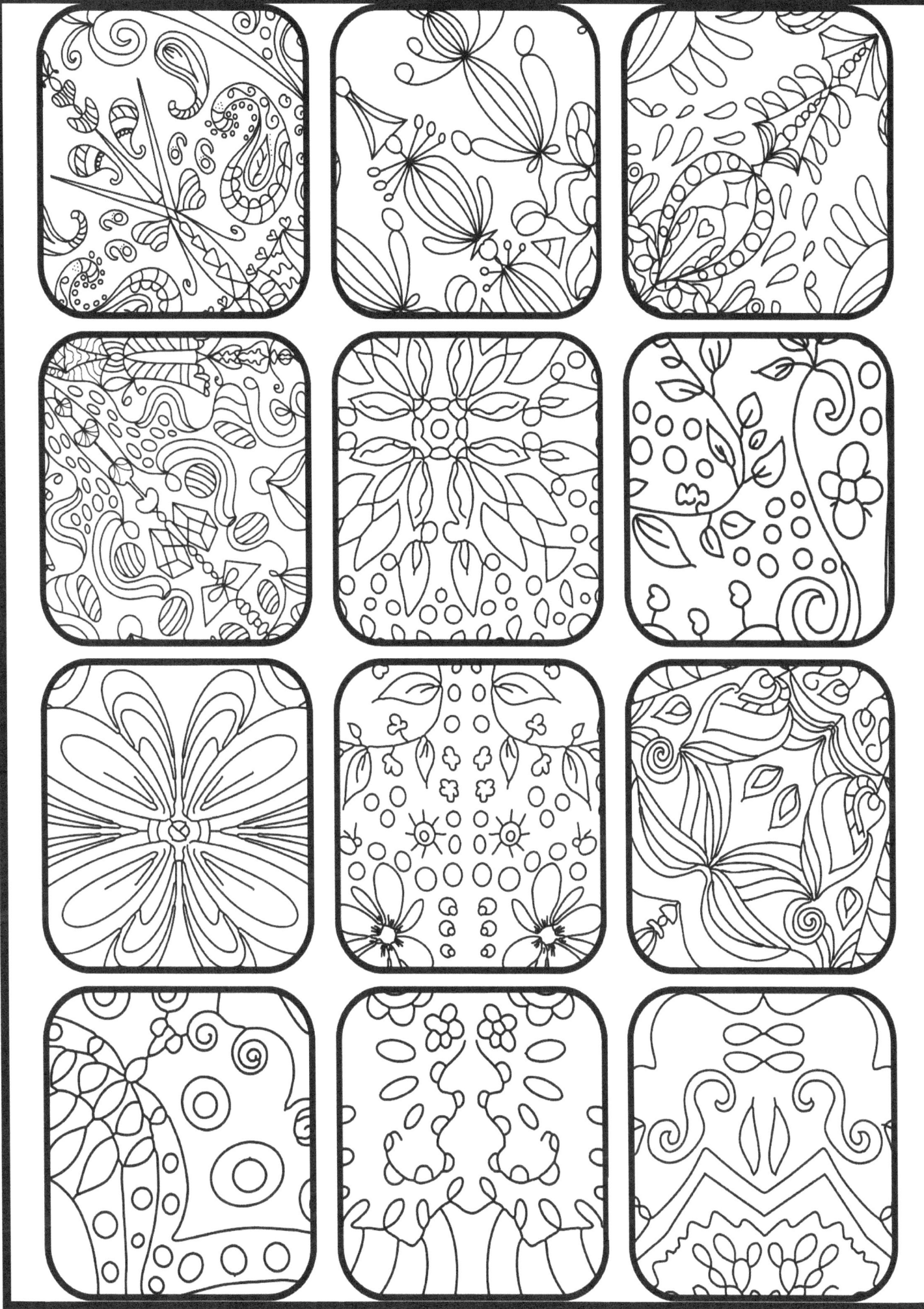

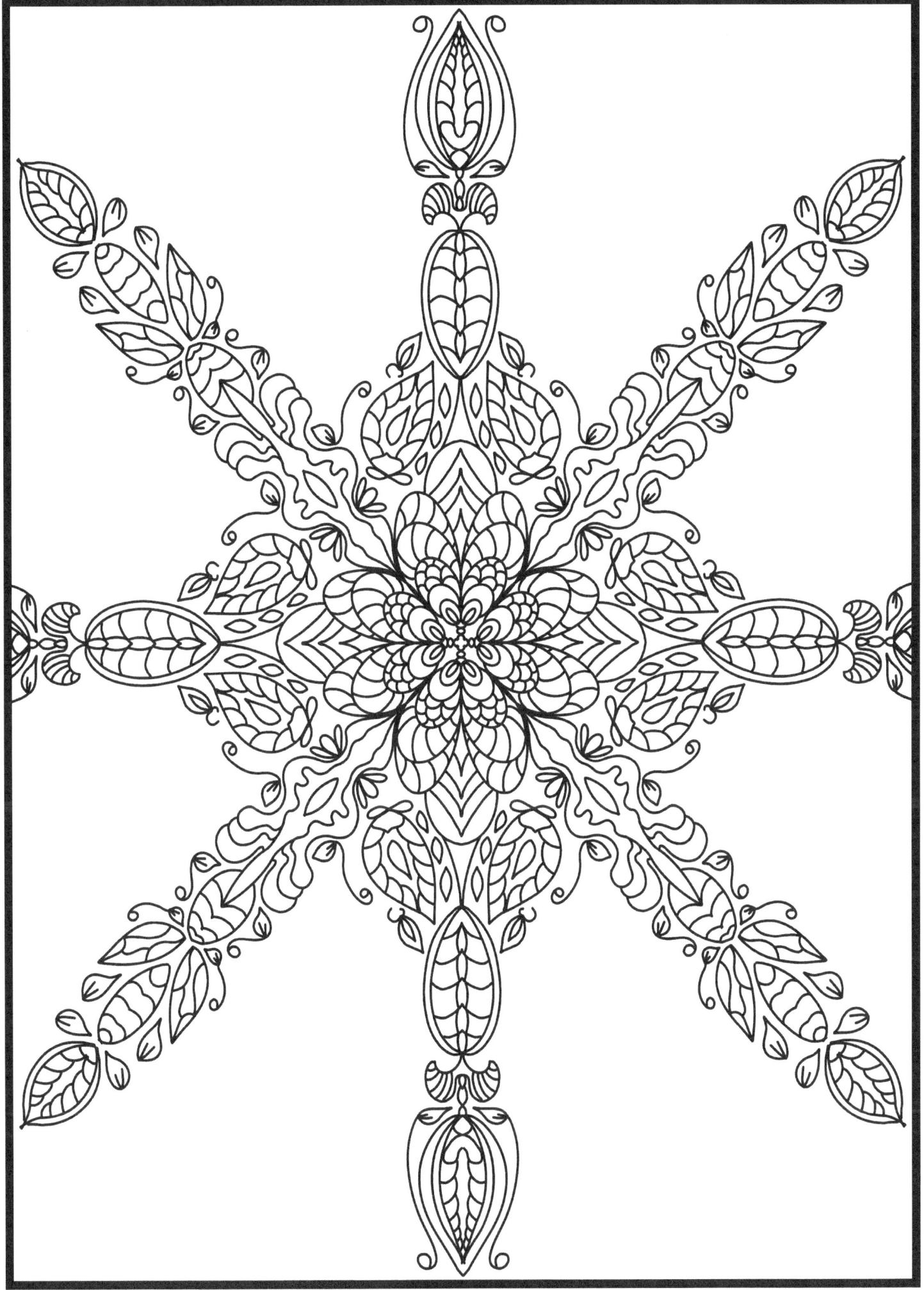

Snowflakes

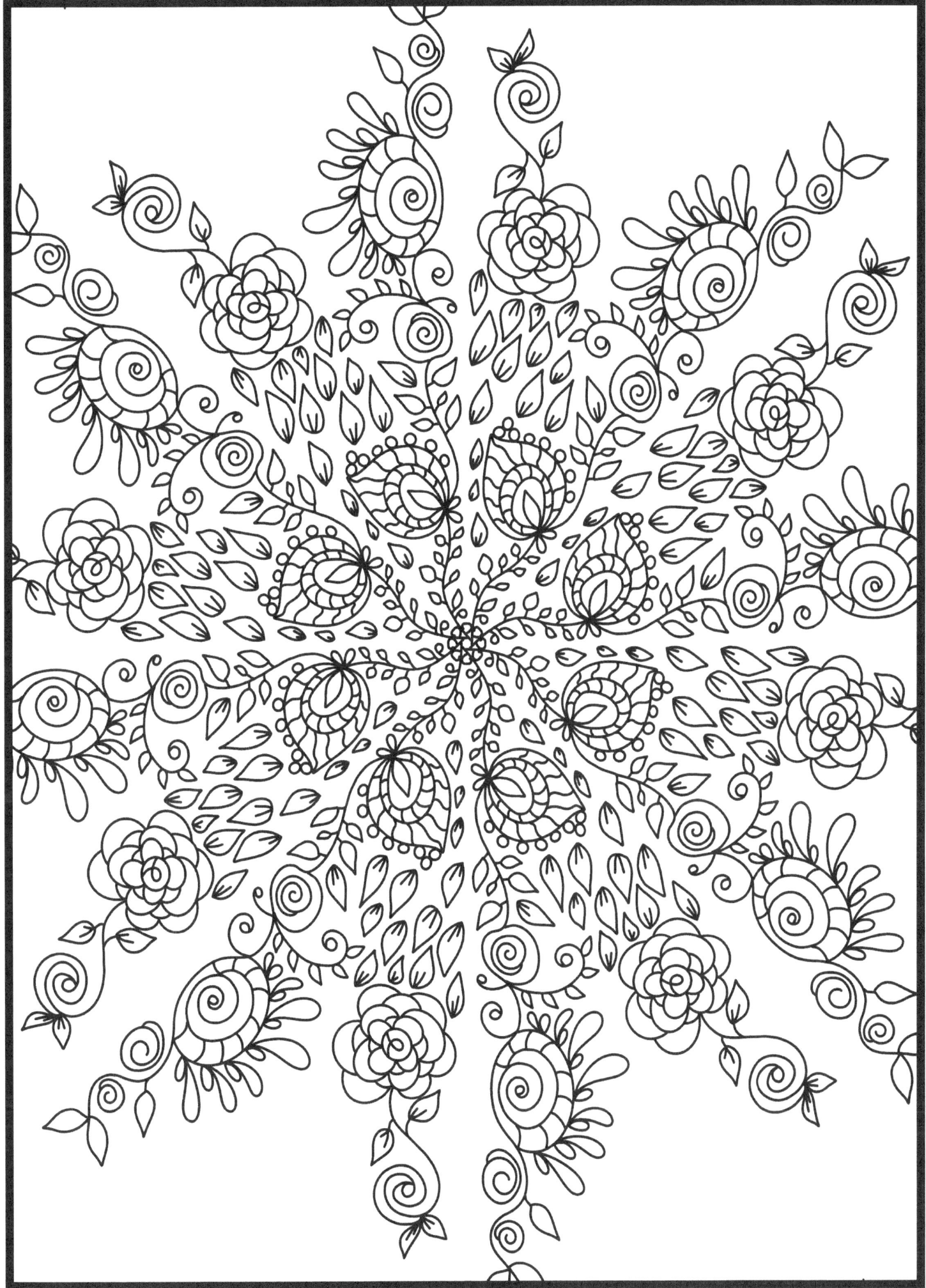

Emerald Forest

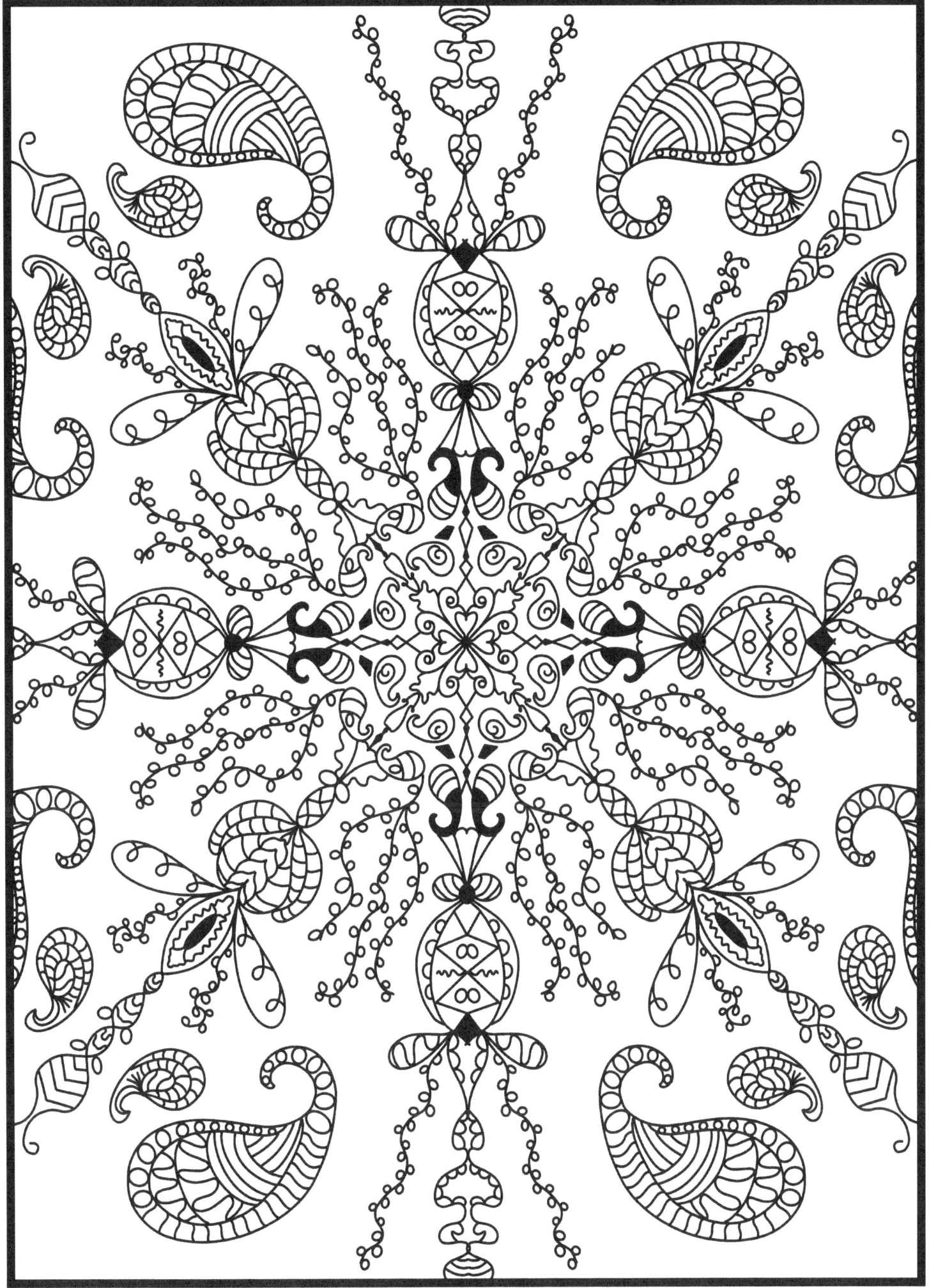

Paradise

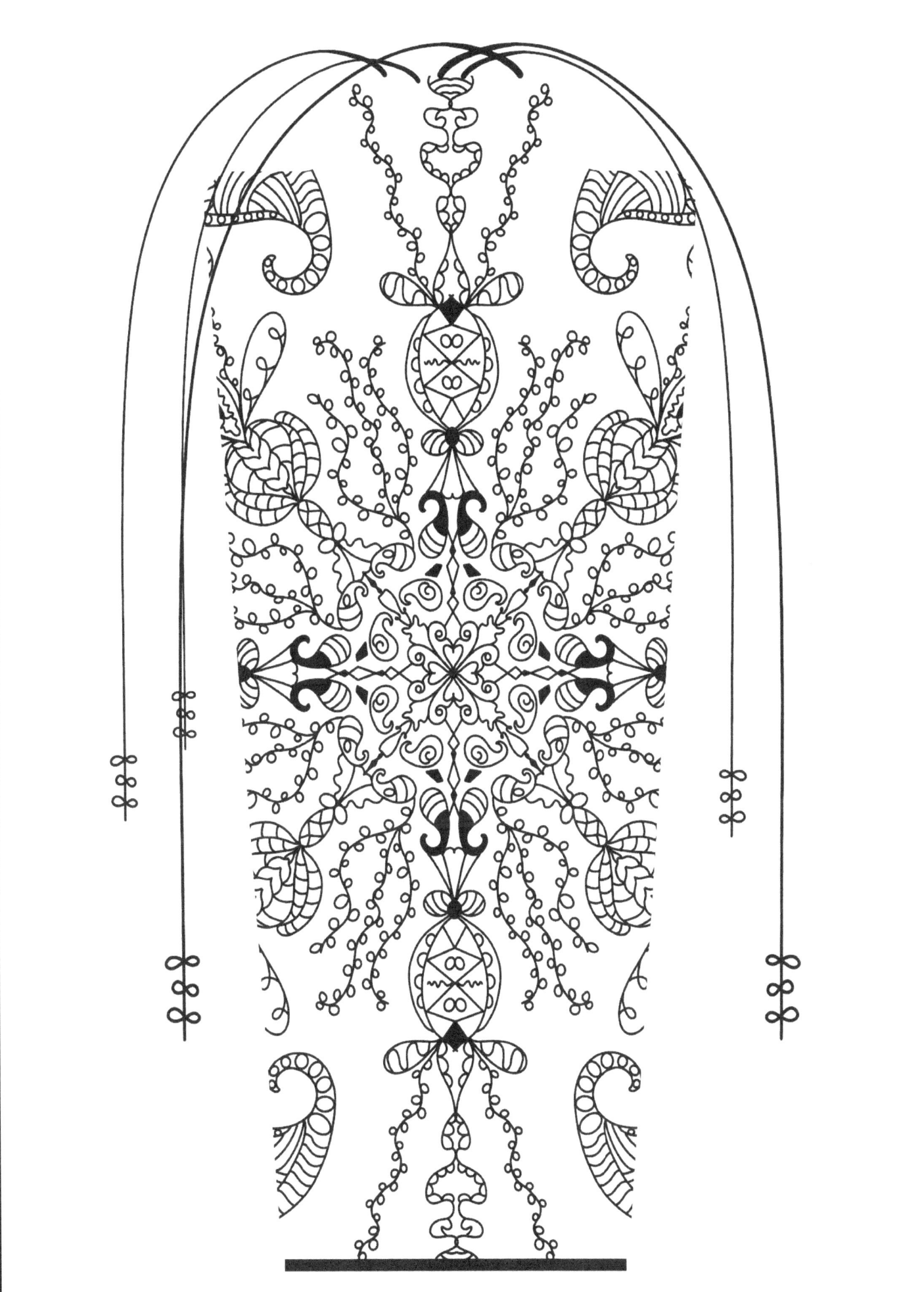

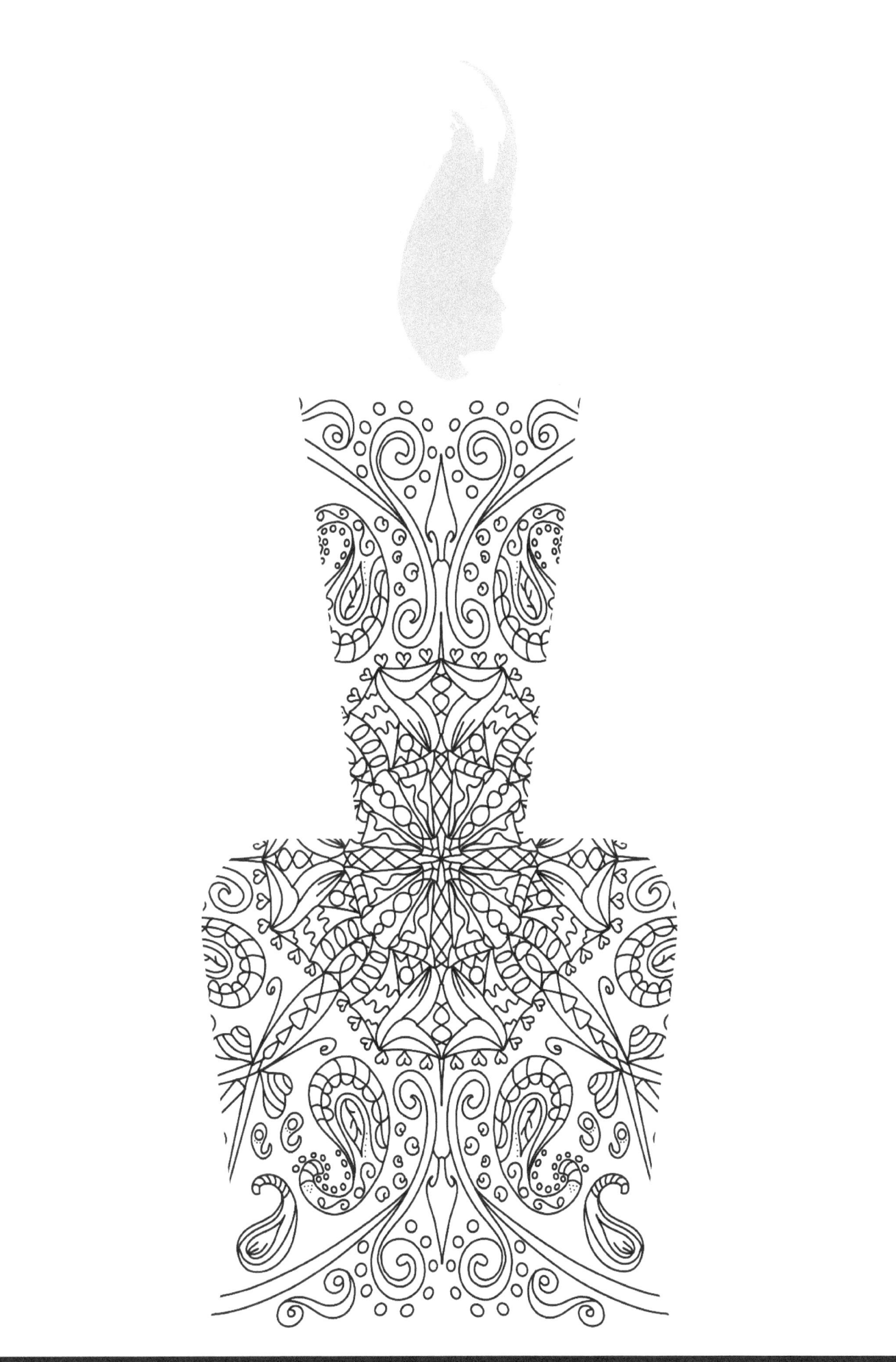

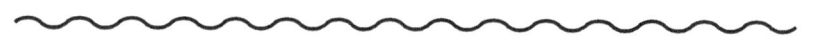

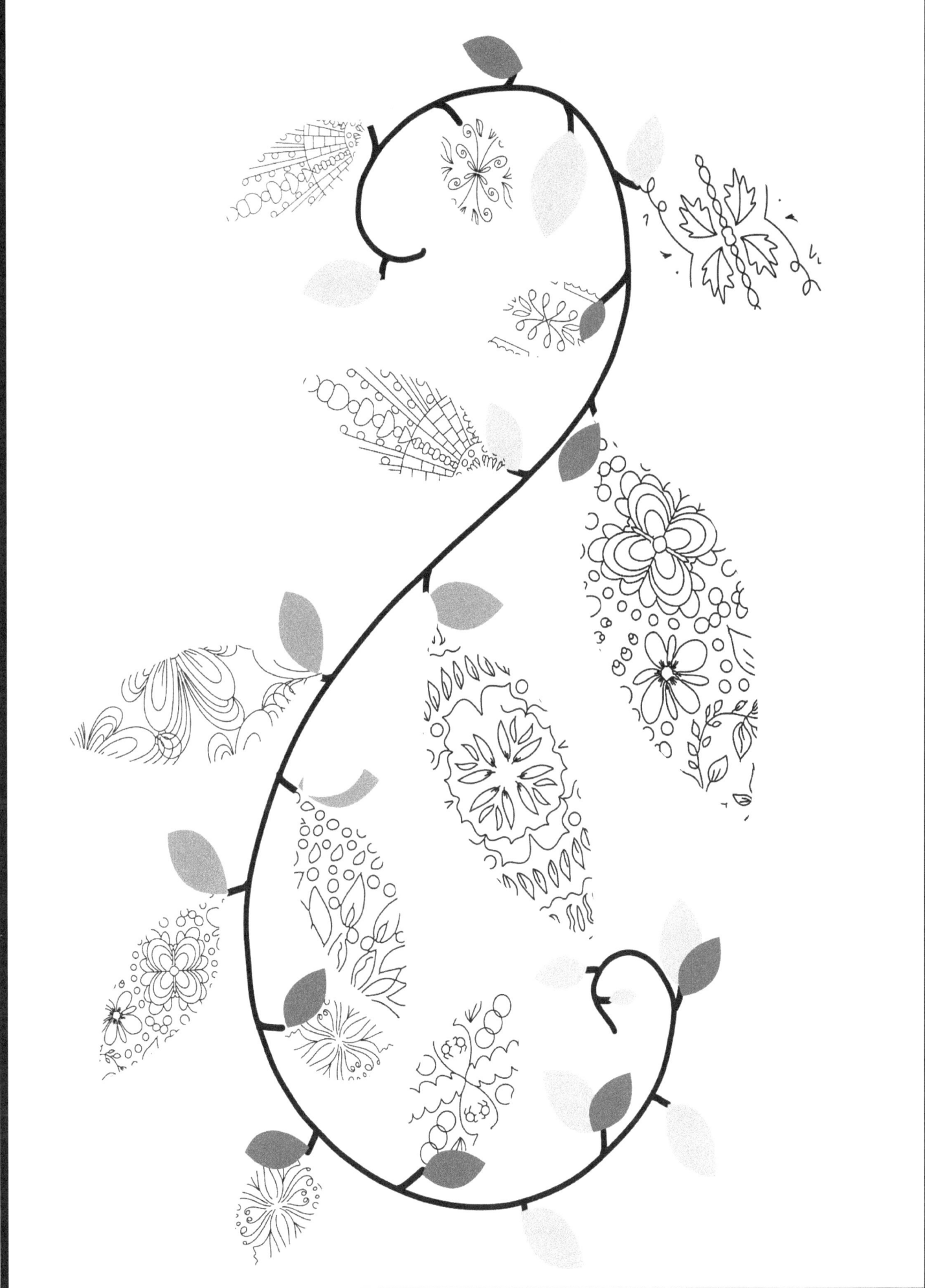

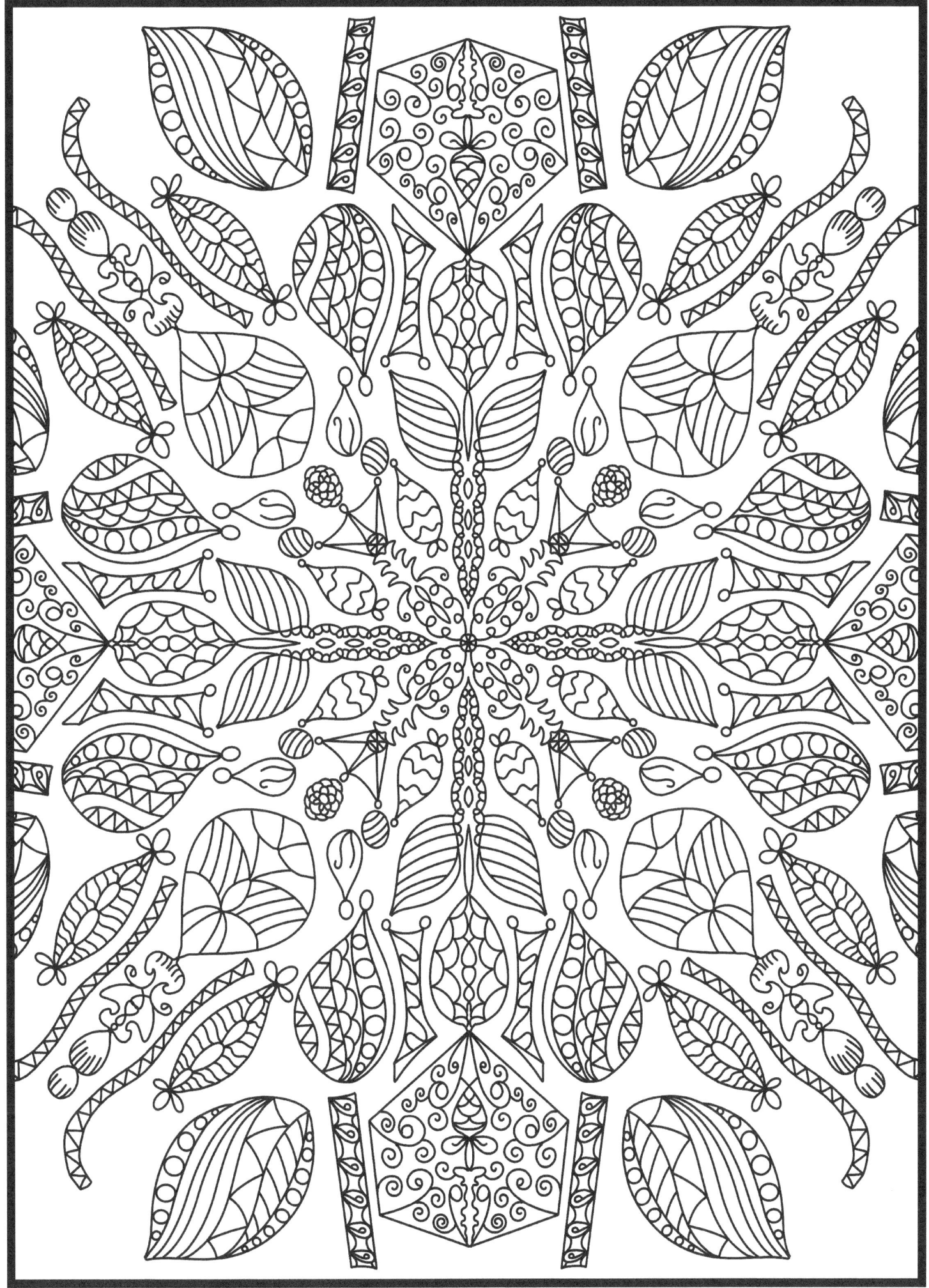

Mandala Yard

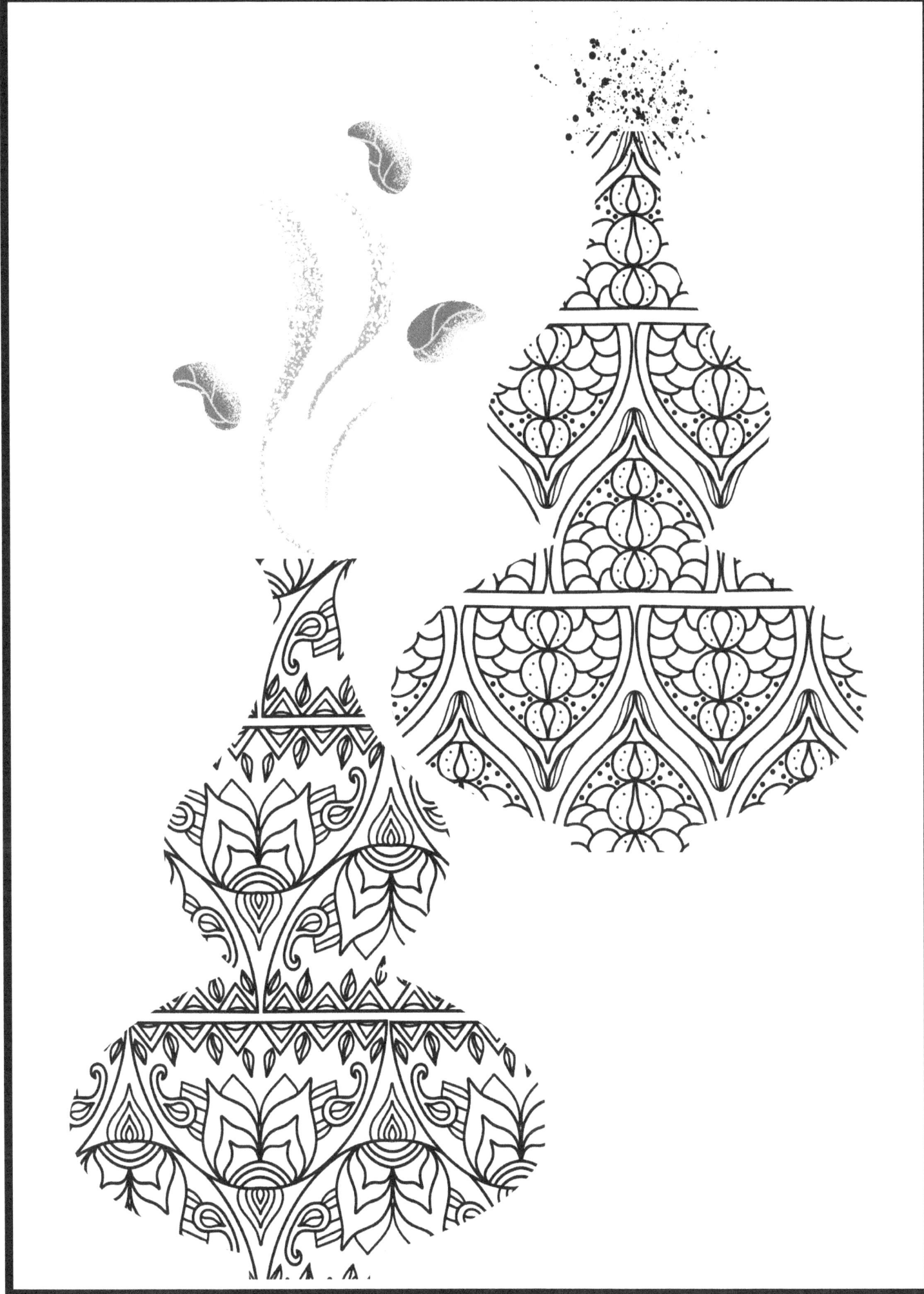

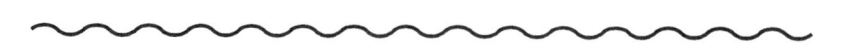

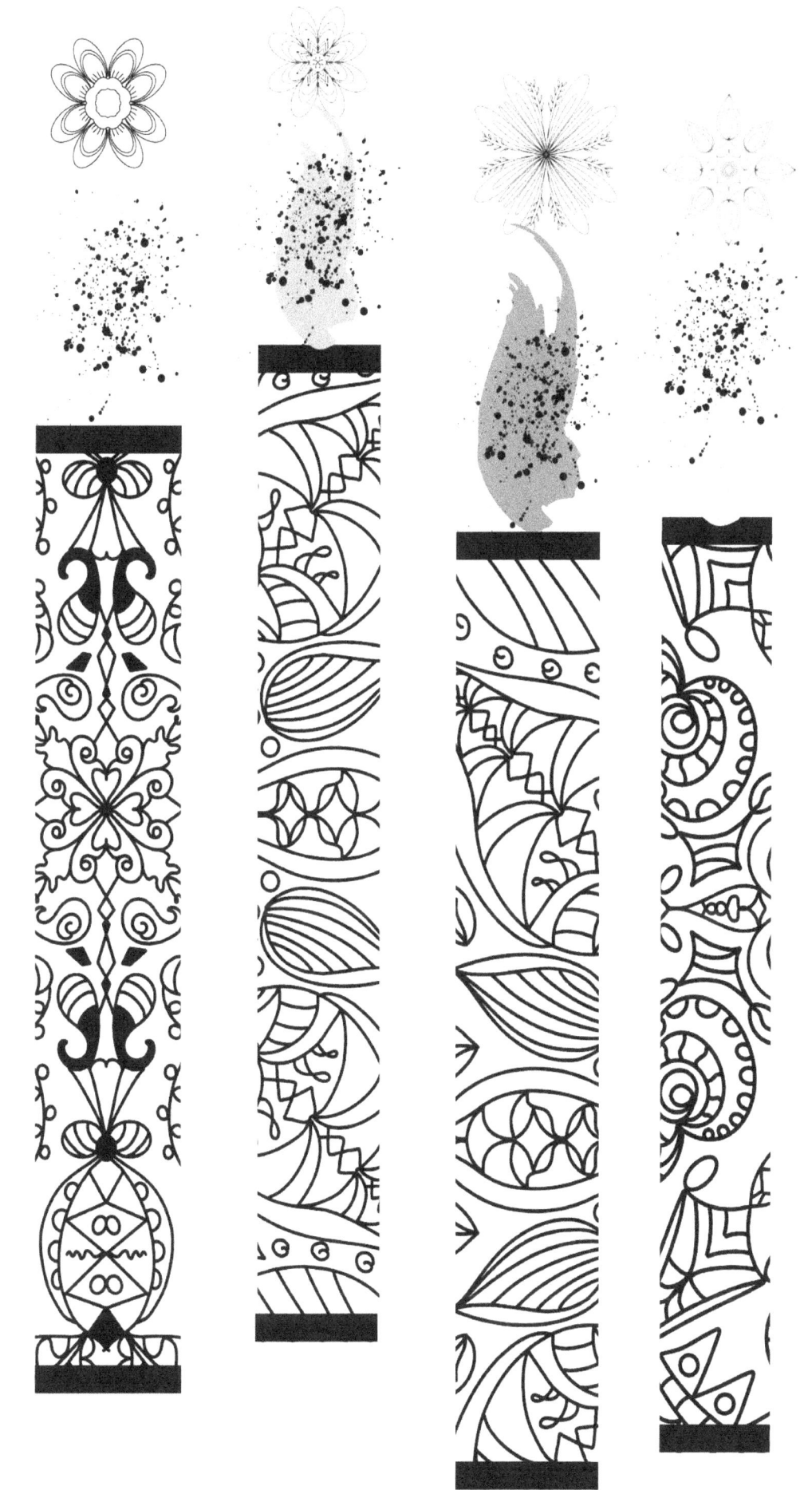

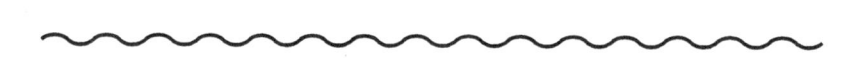

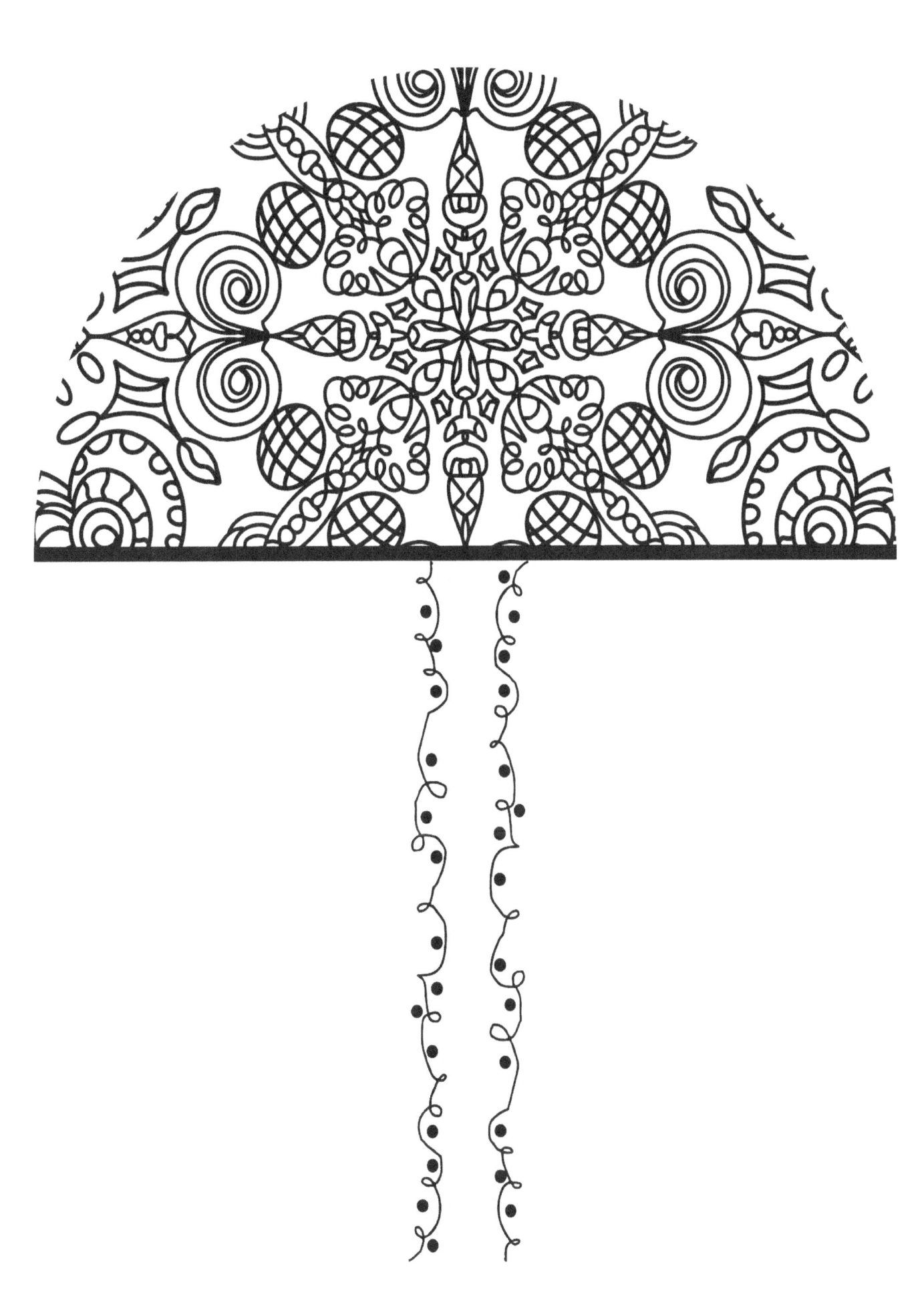

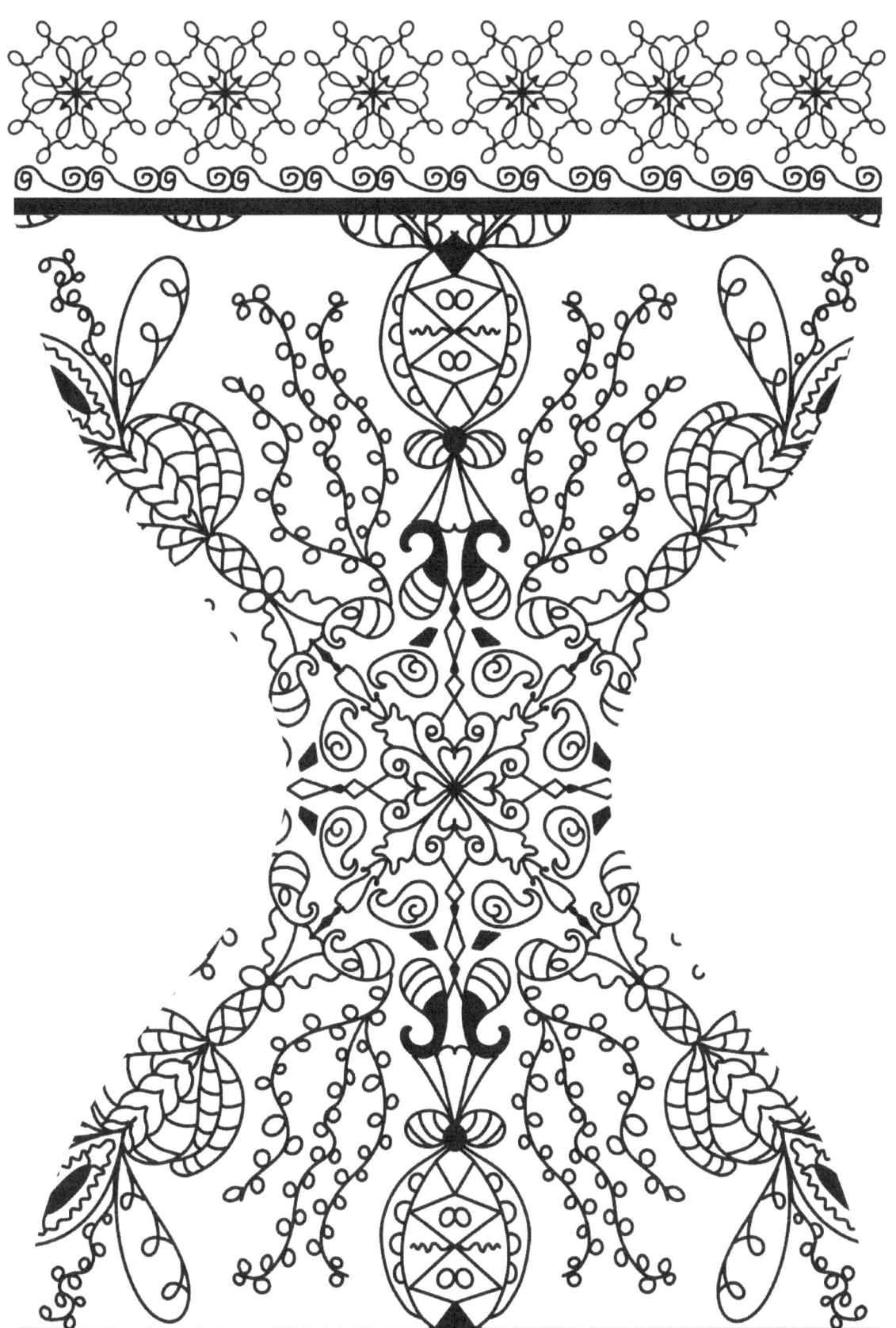

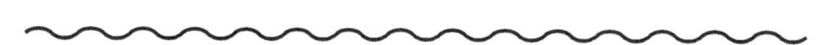

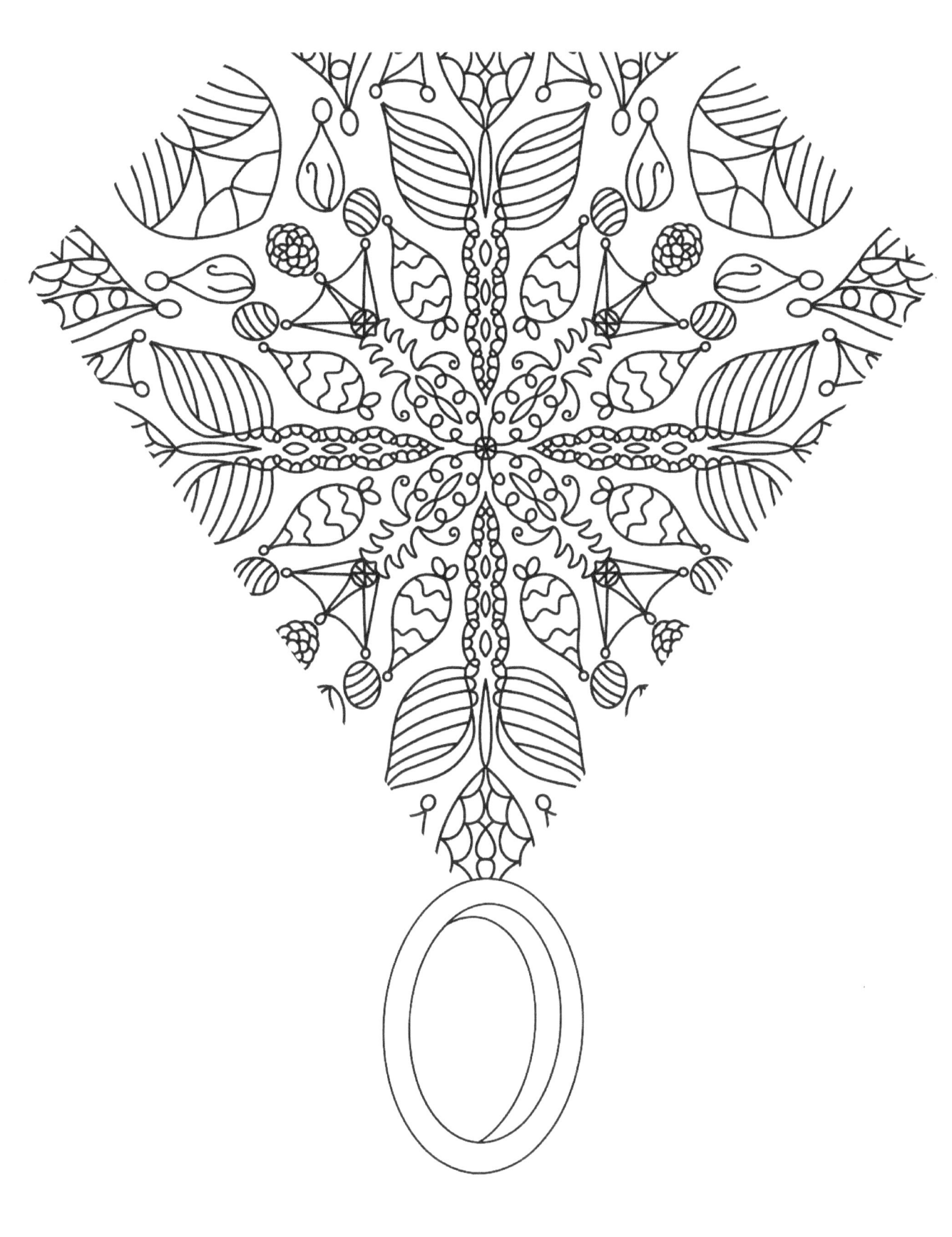

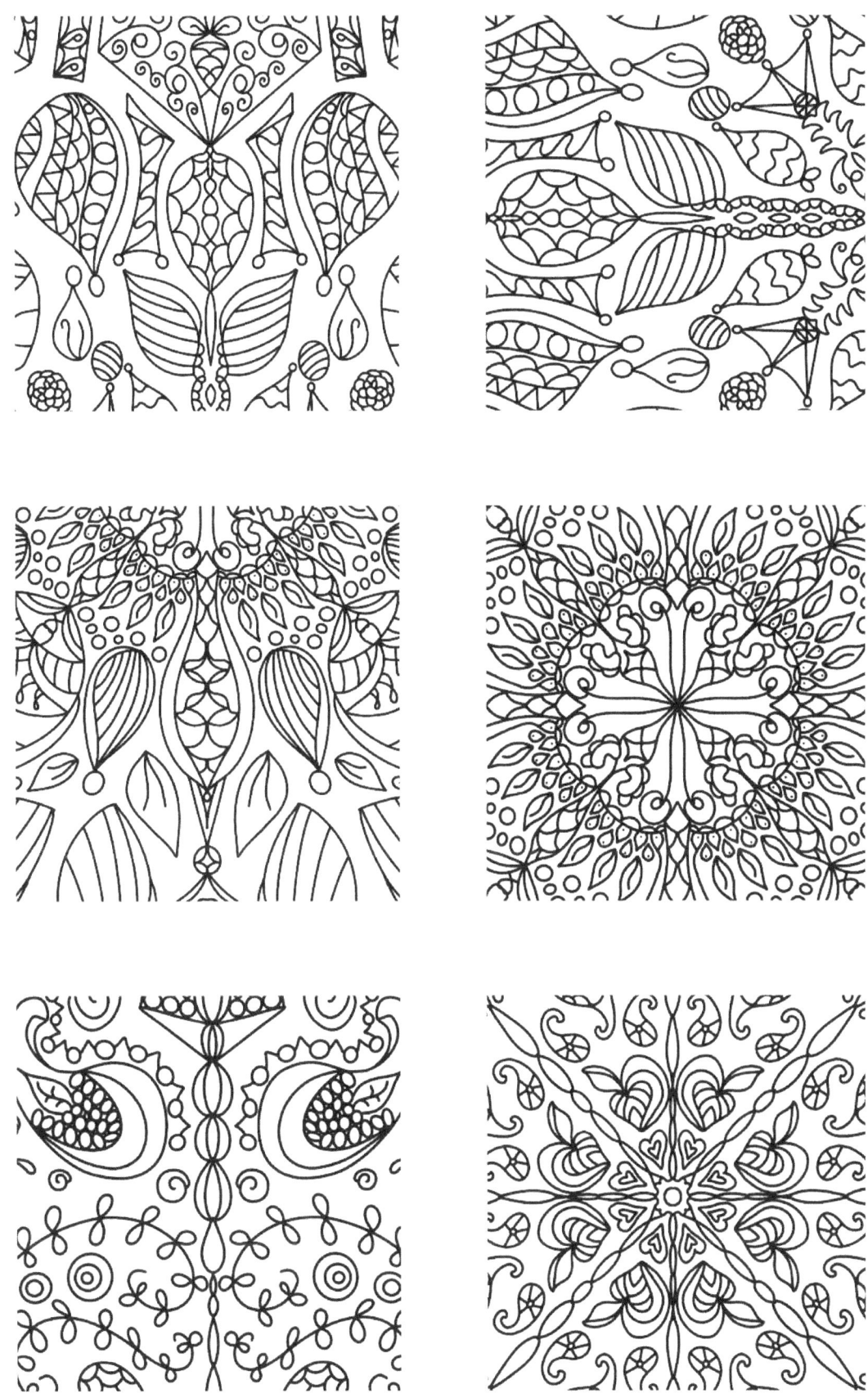

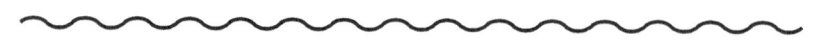

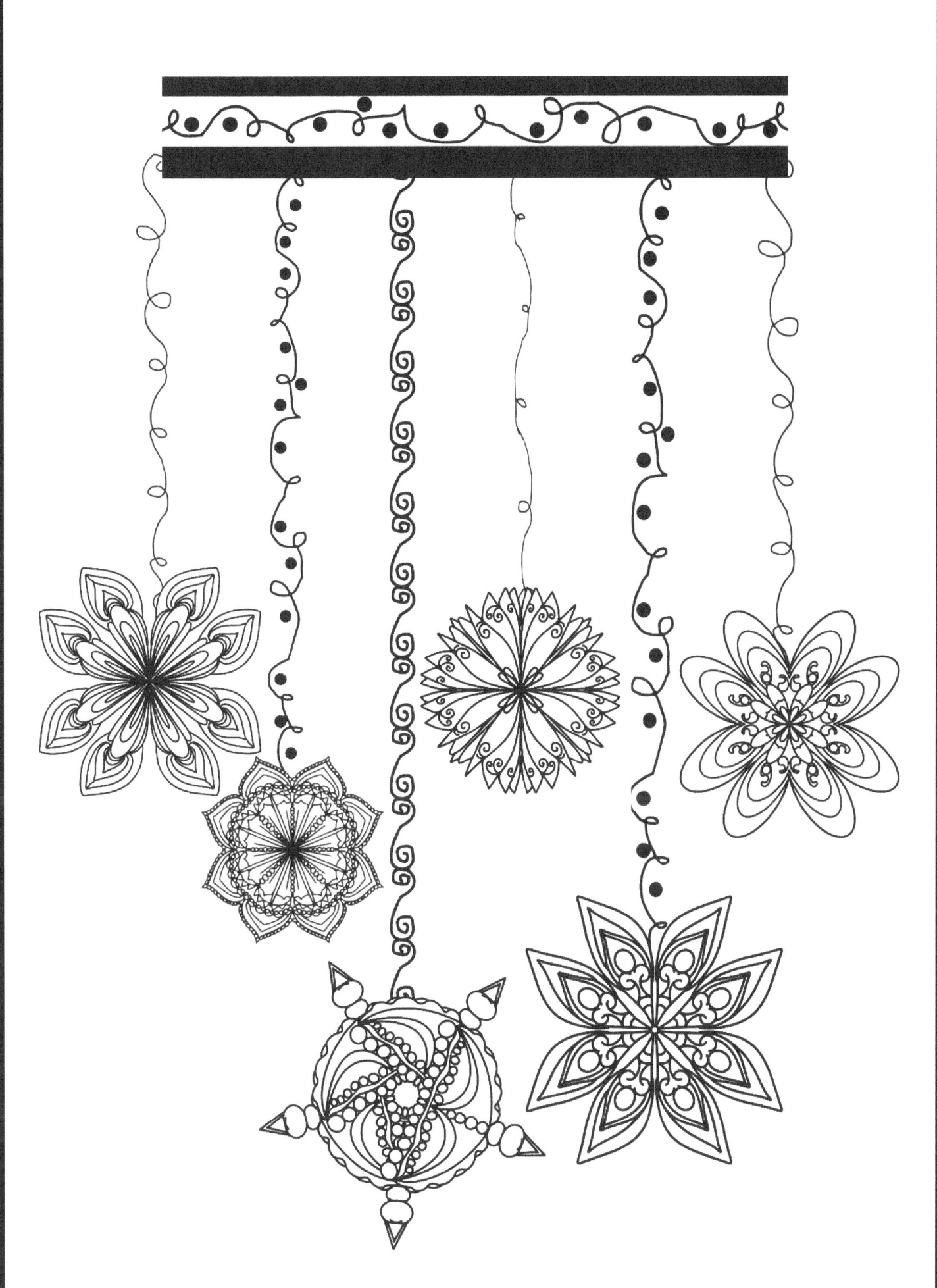

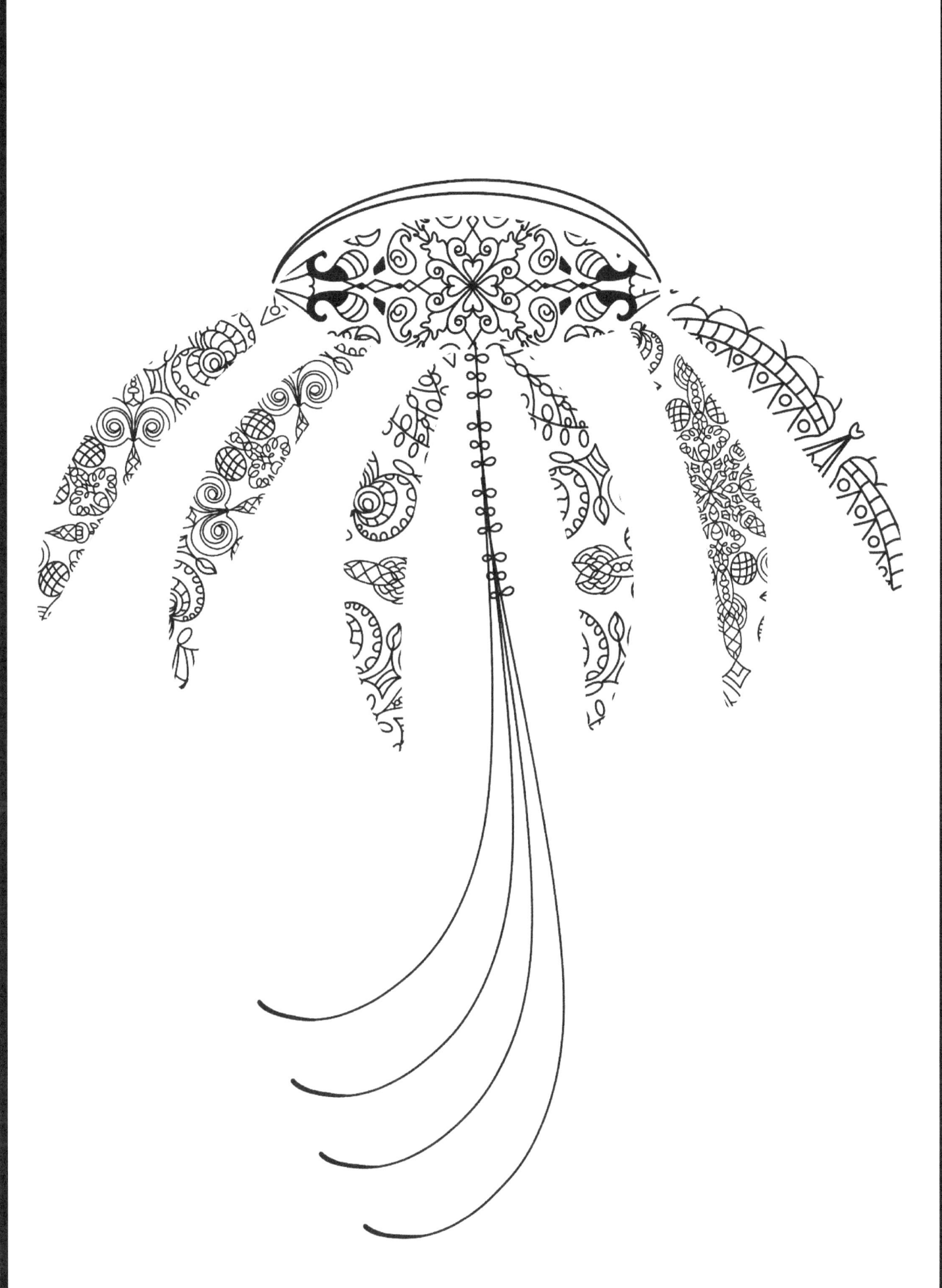

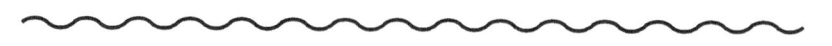

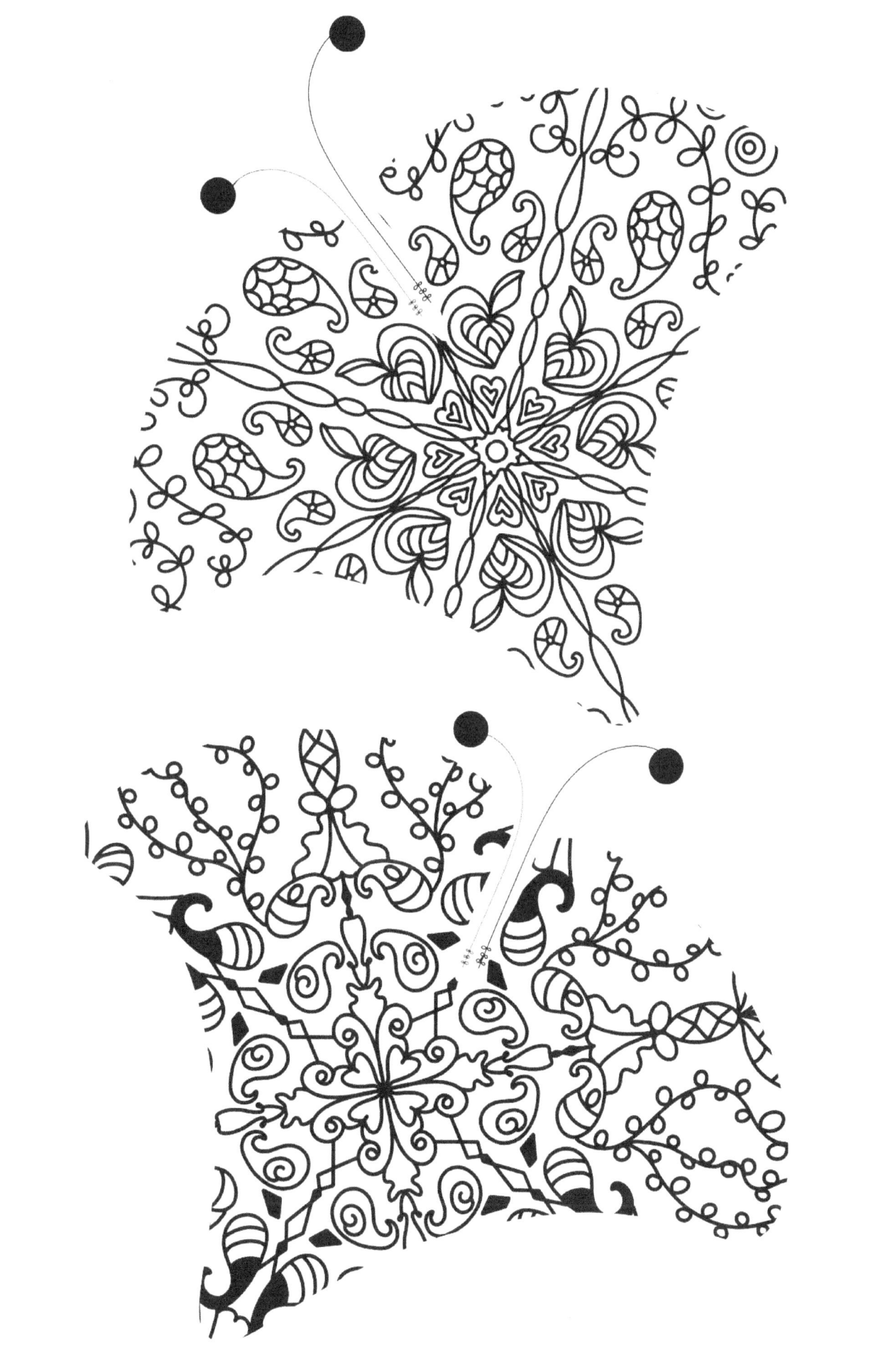

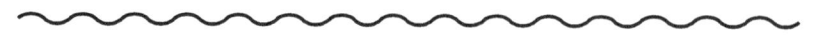

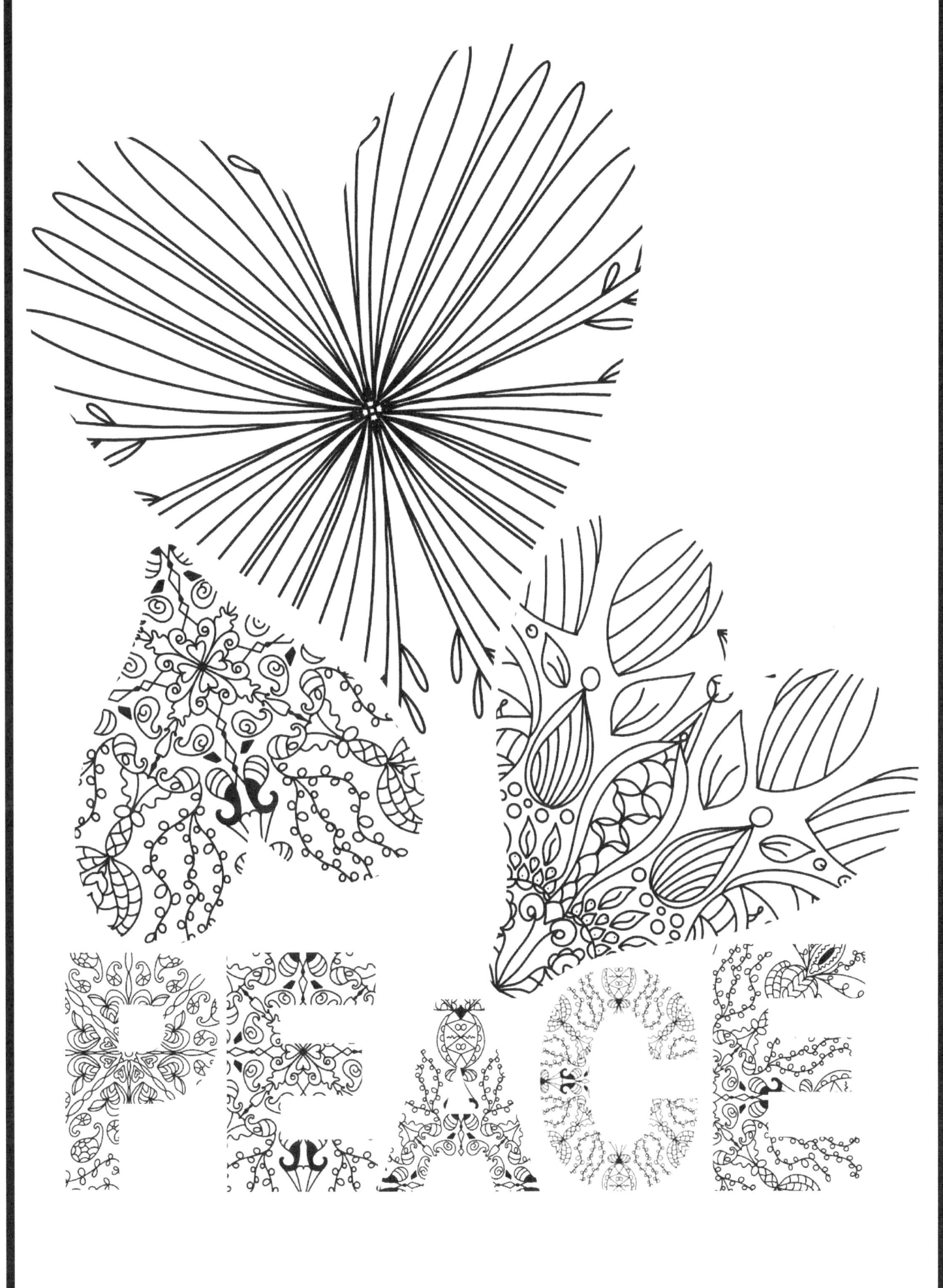

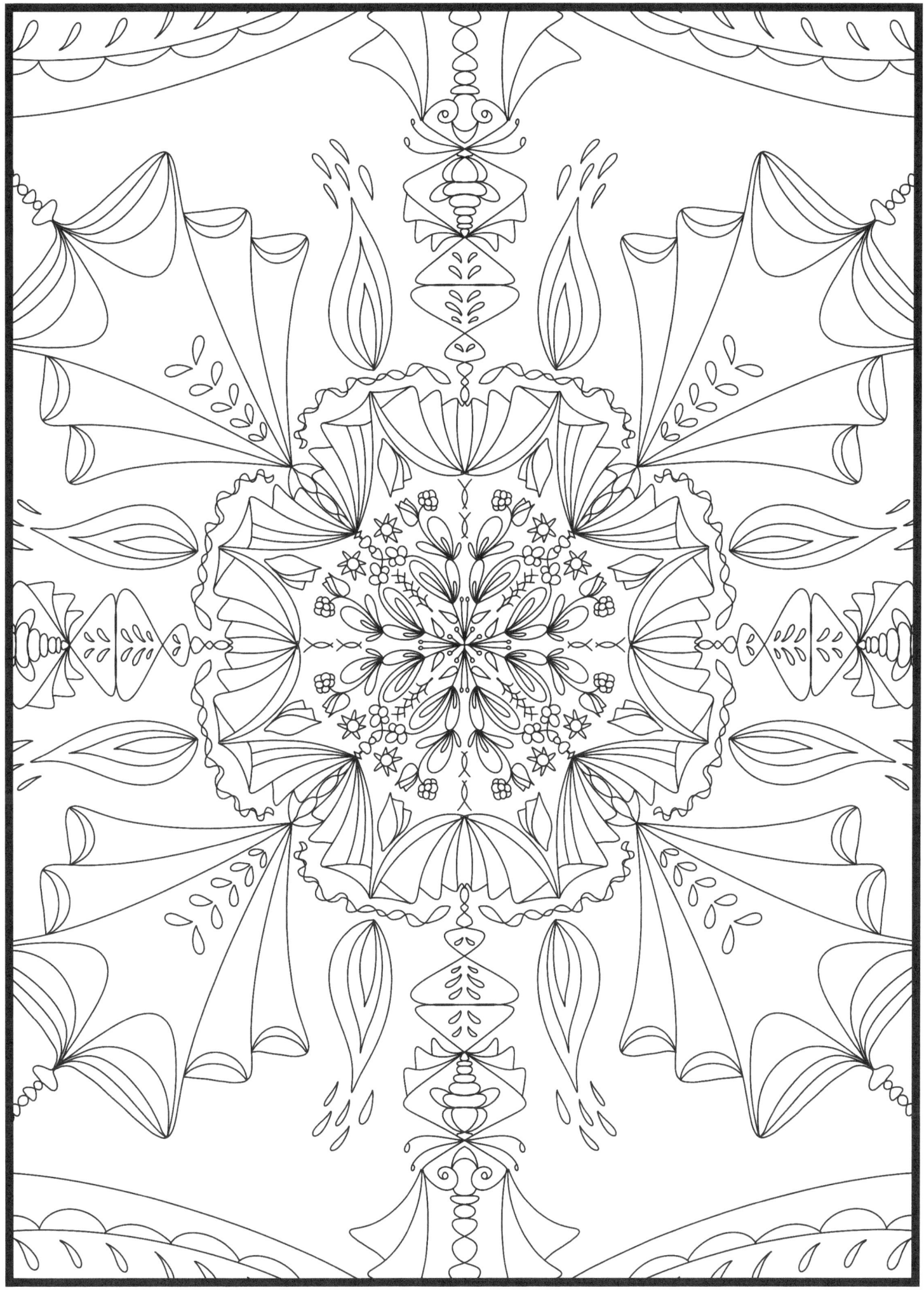

Weekends

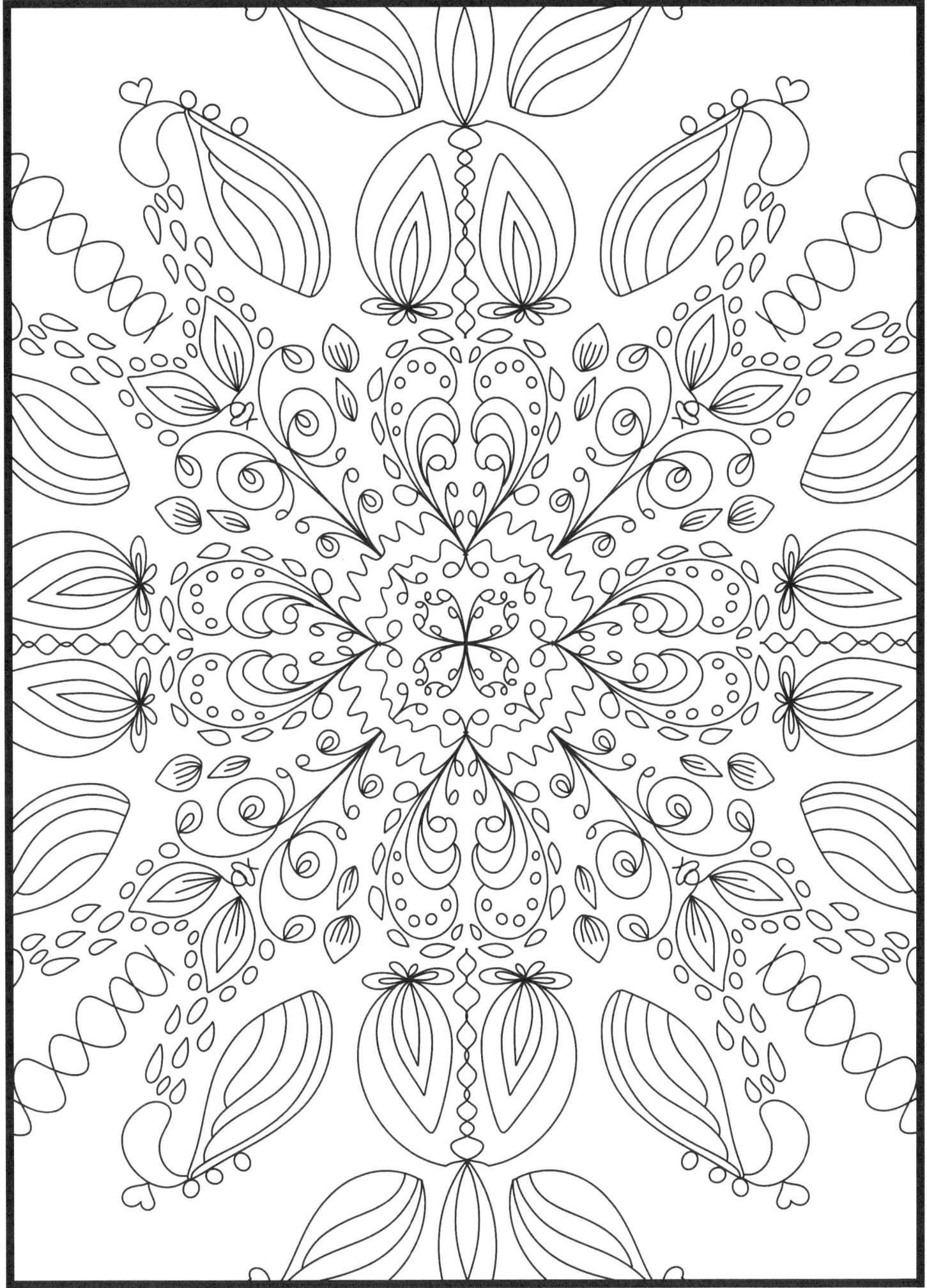

Love
~~~~~~~~~~~~~~~~~~~~~~~~~~~

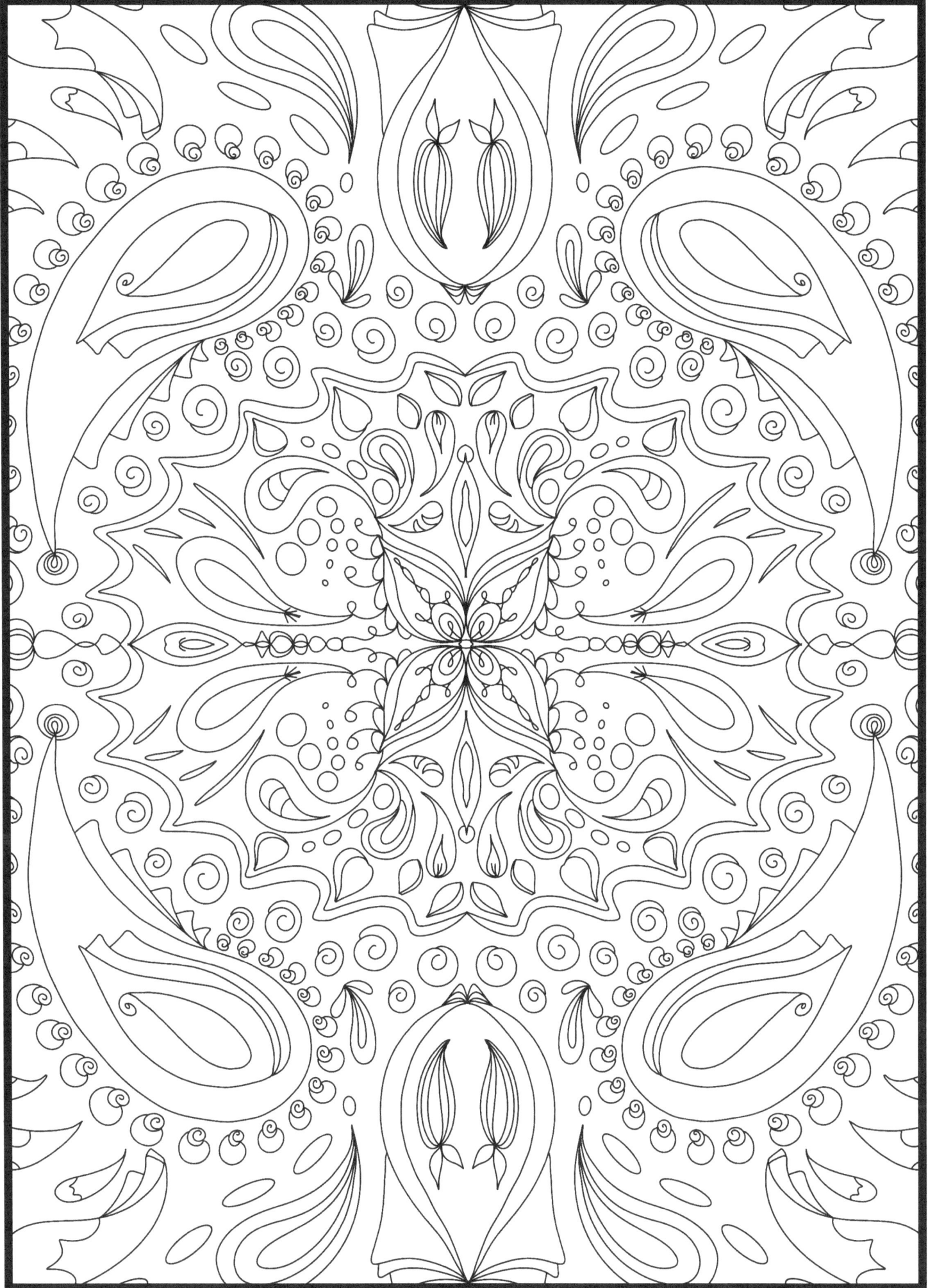

Joy

~~~~~~~~~~~~~~~~~~~~~~~

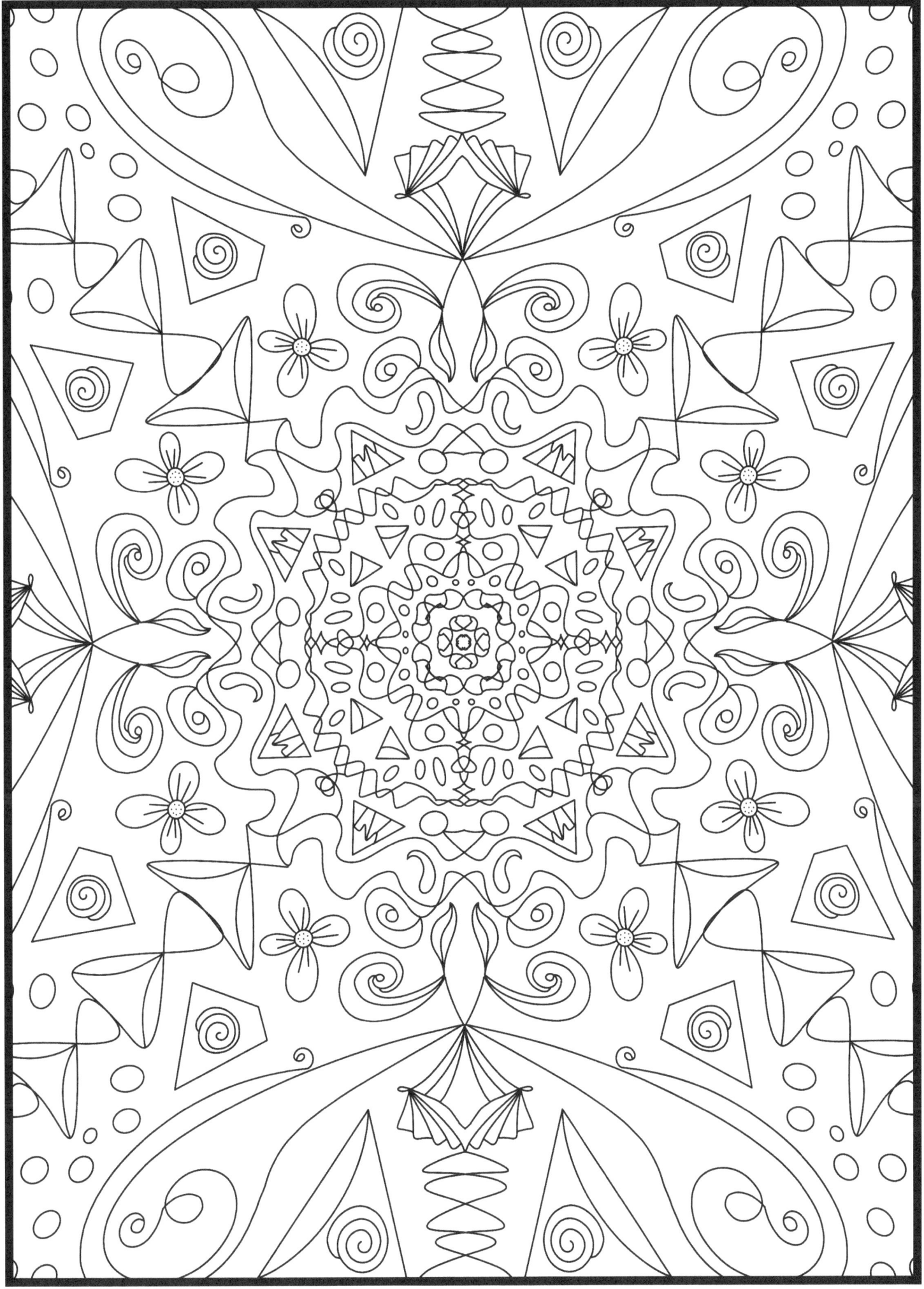

Family

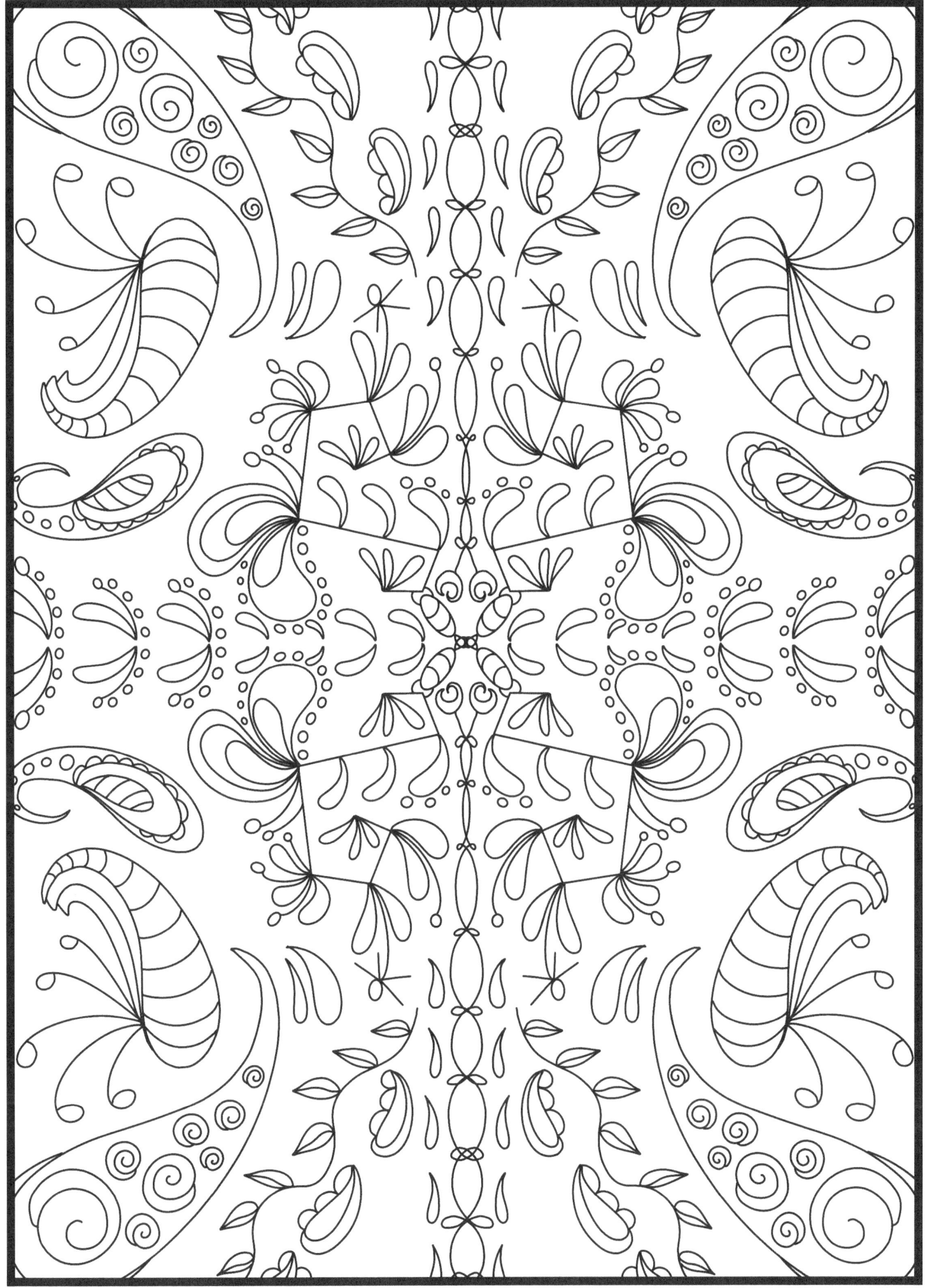

Winter Calm

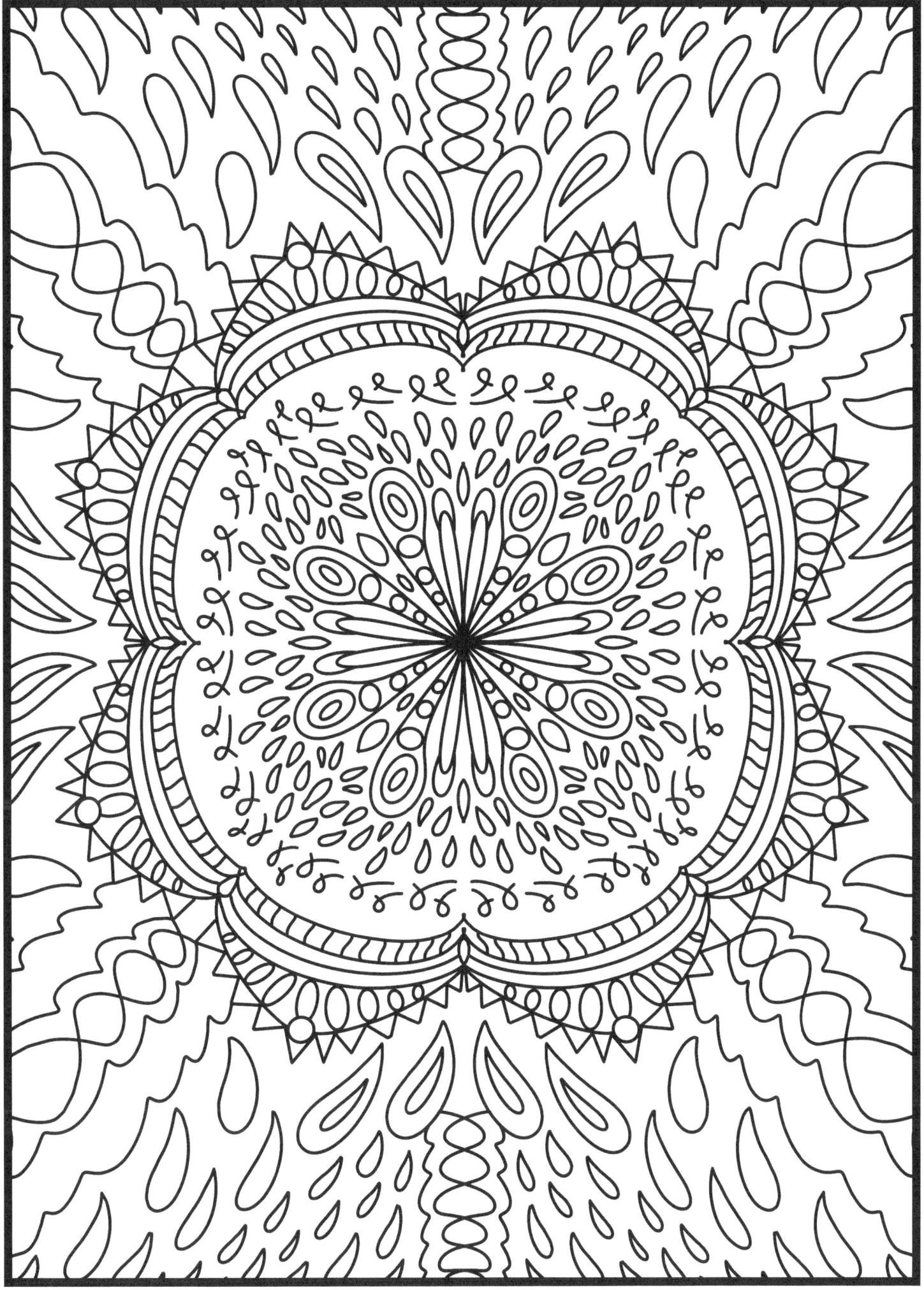

Wild Gardens

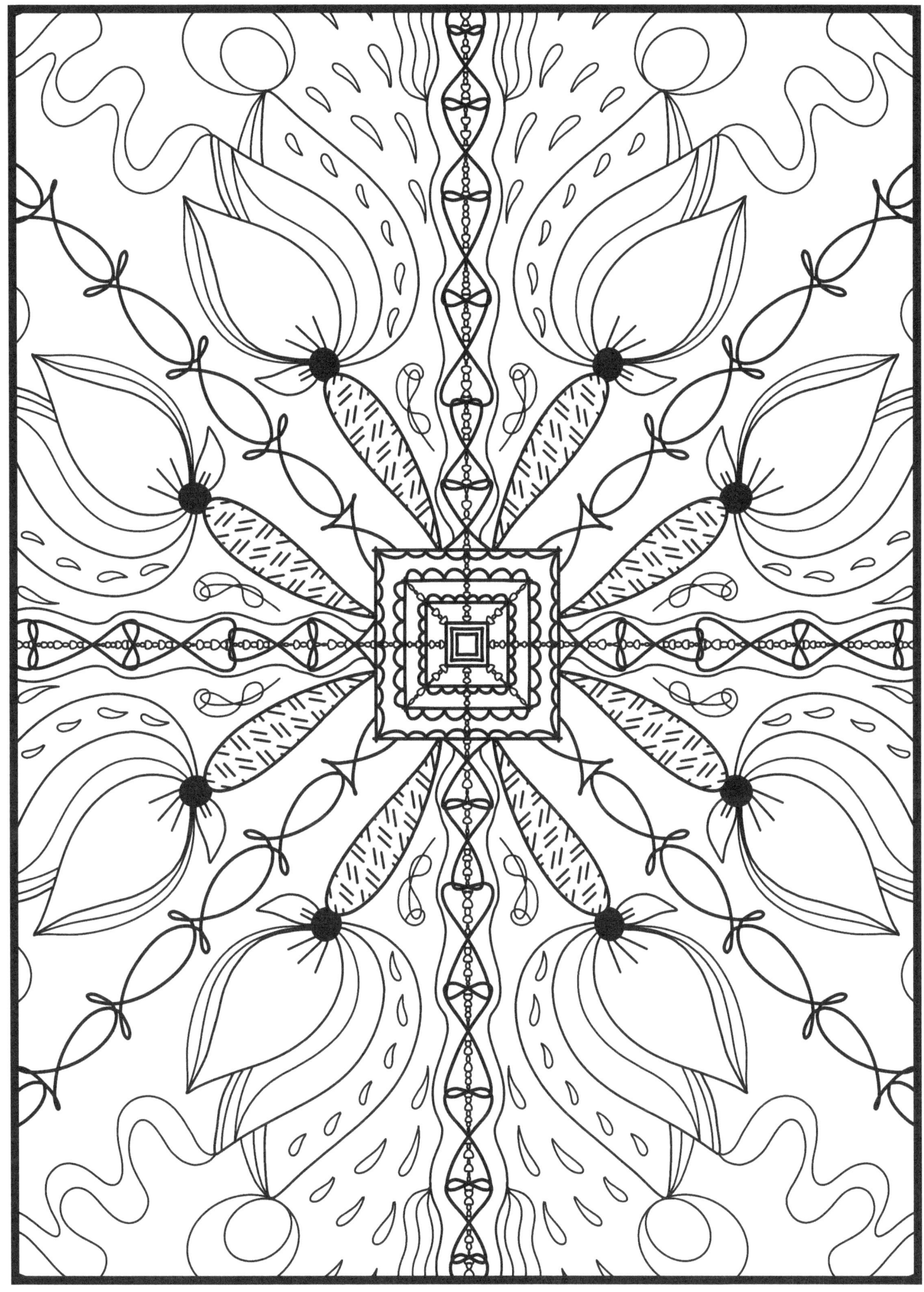

Tropical Islands

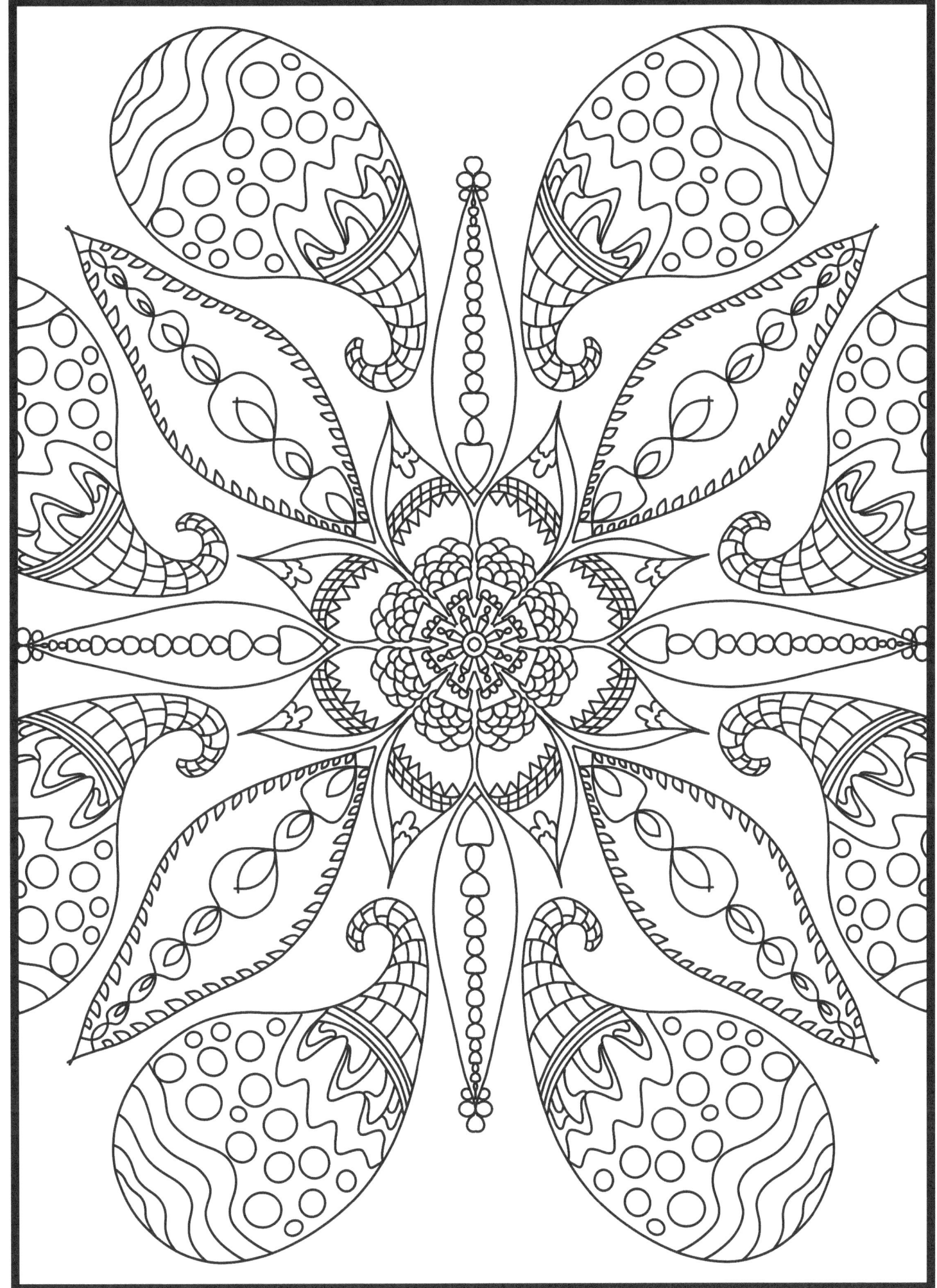

Simple Time

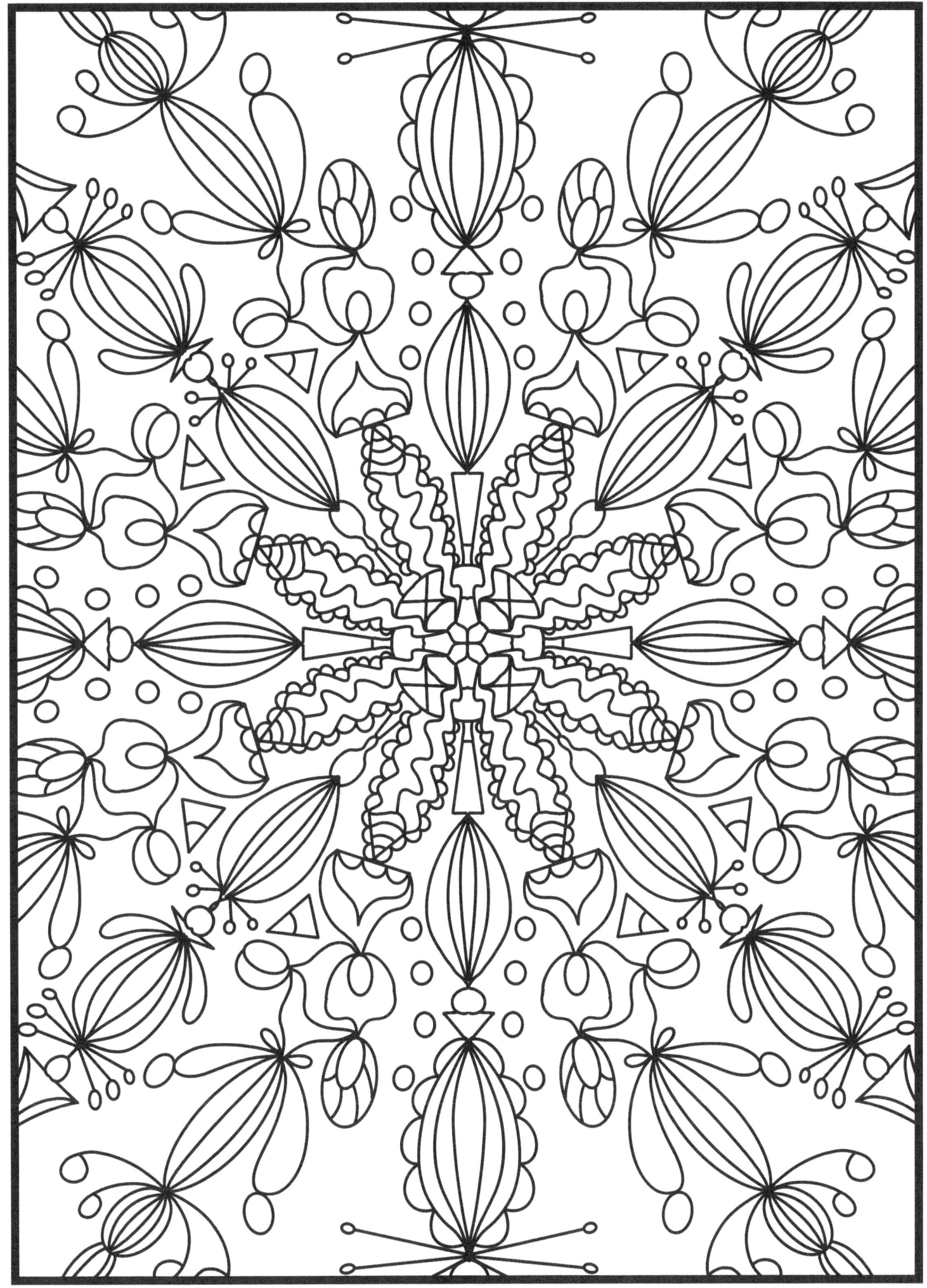

Floral Blooms

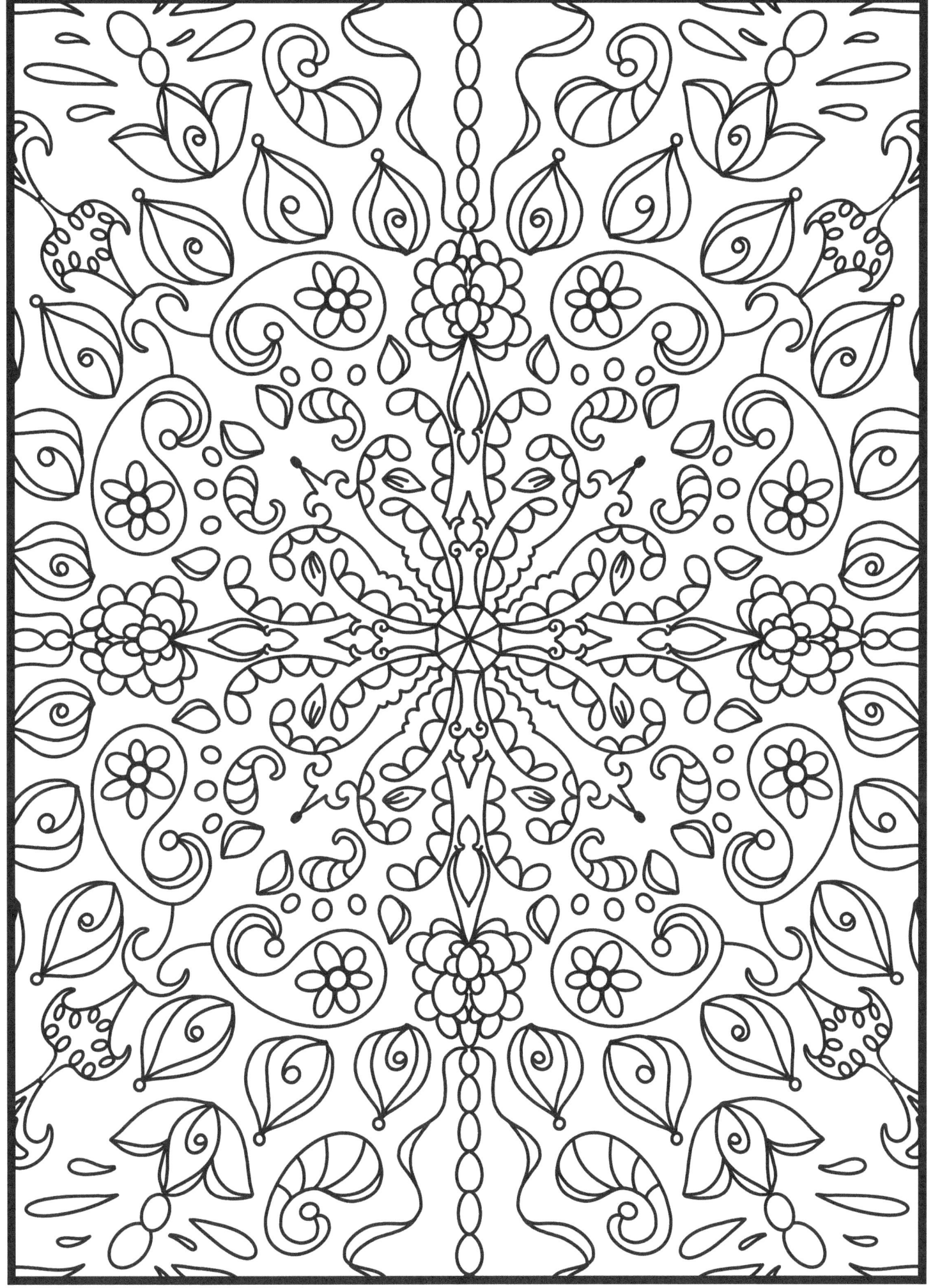

Sunny Sunrise

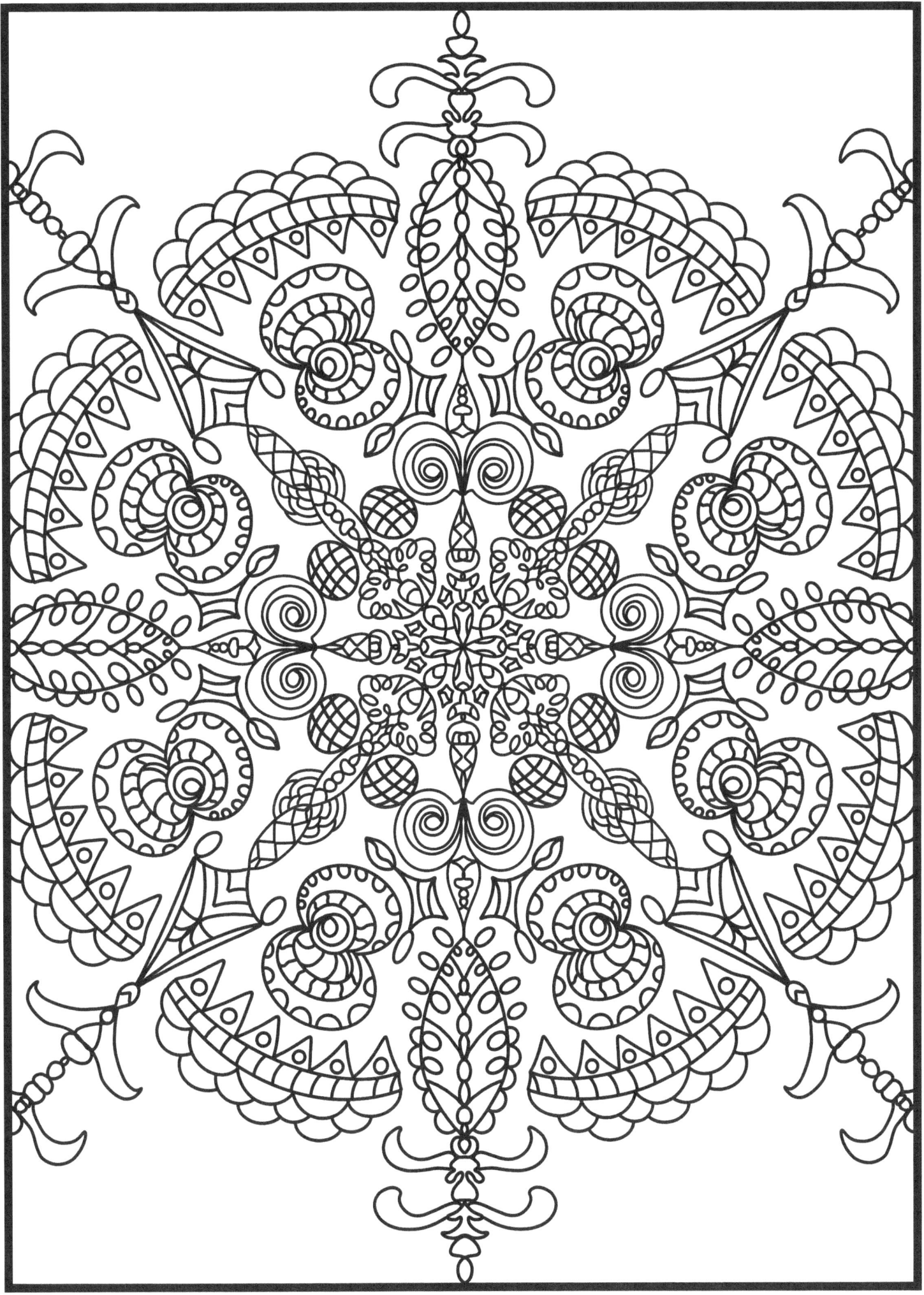

Jade Gardens

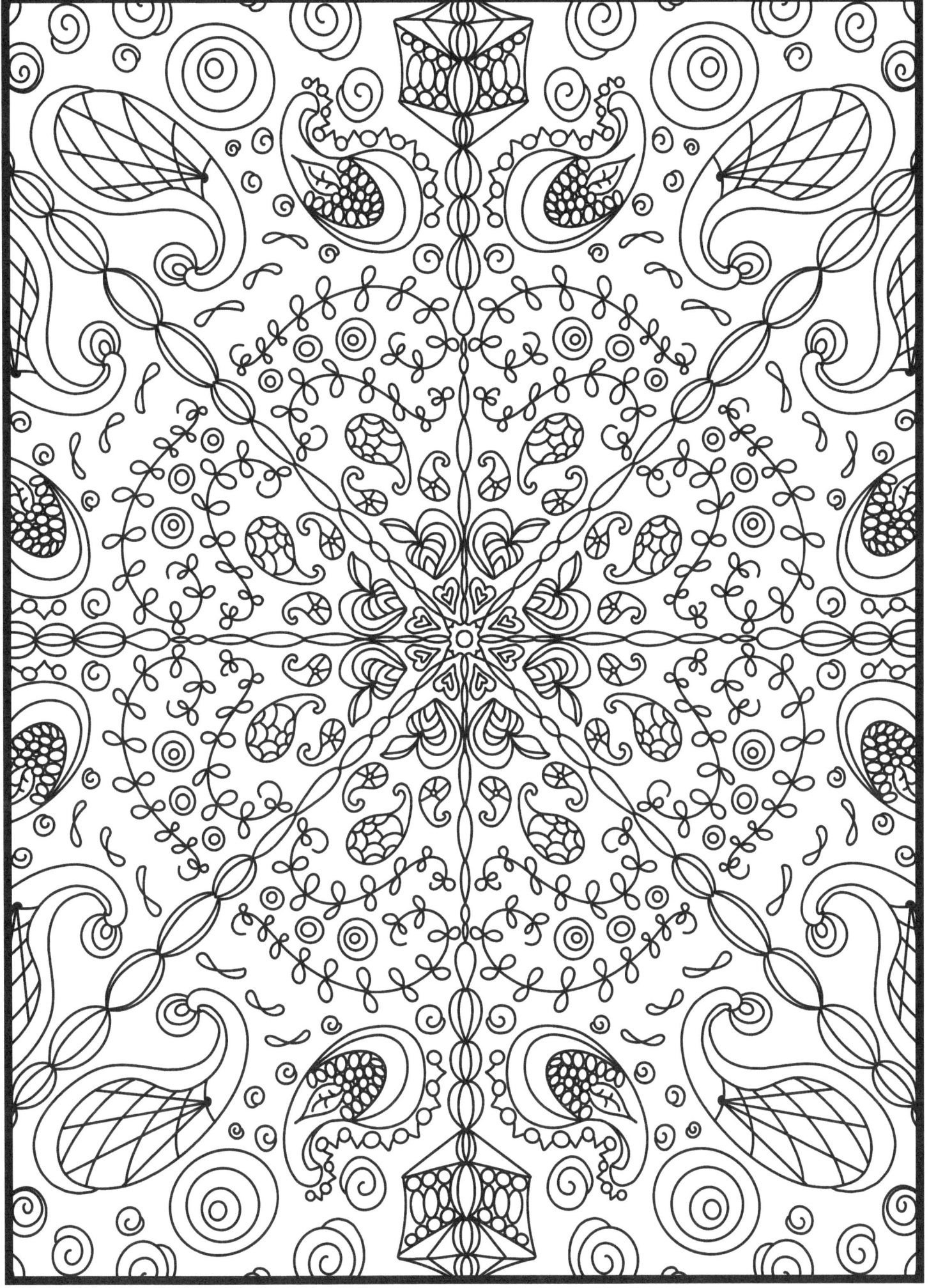

Quilt Blankets

Calm Gardens

Tropical Rain

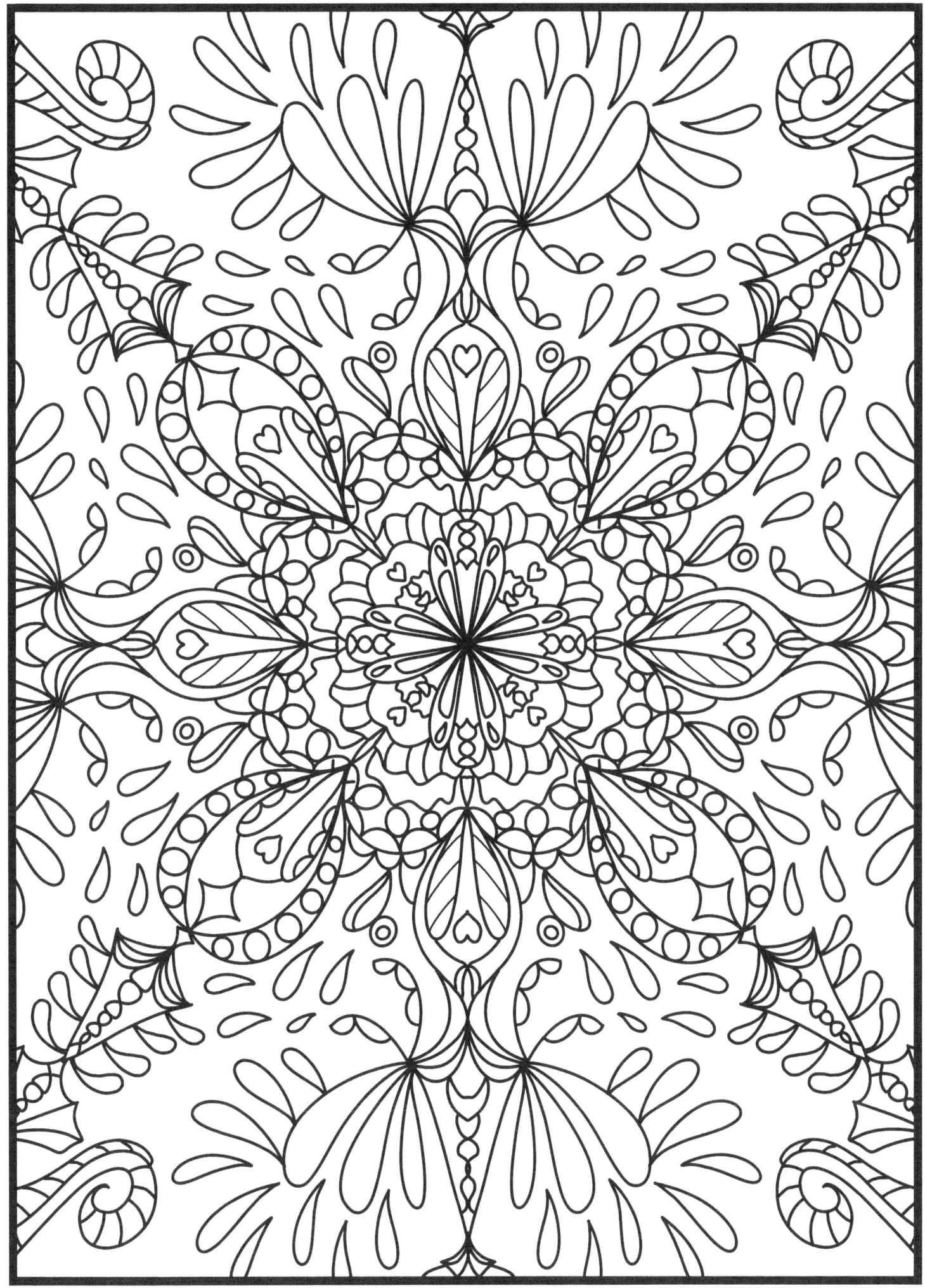

//

Lotus Medley

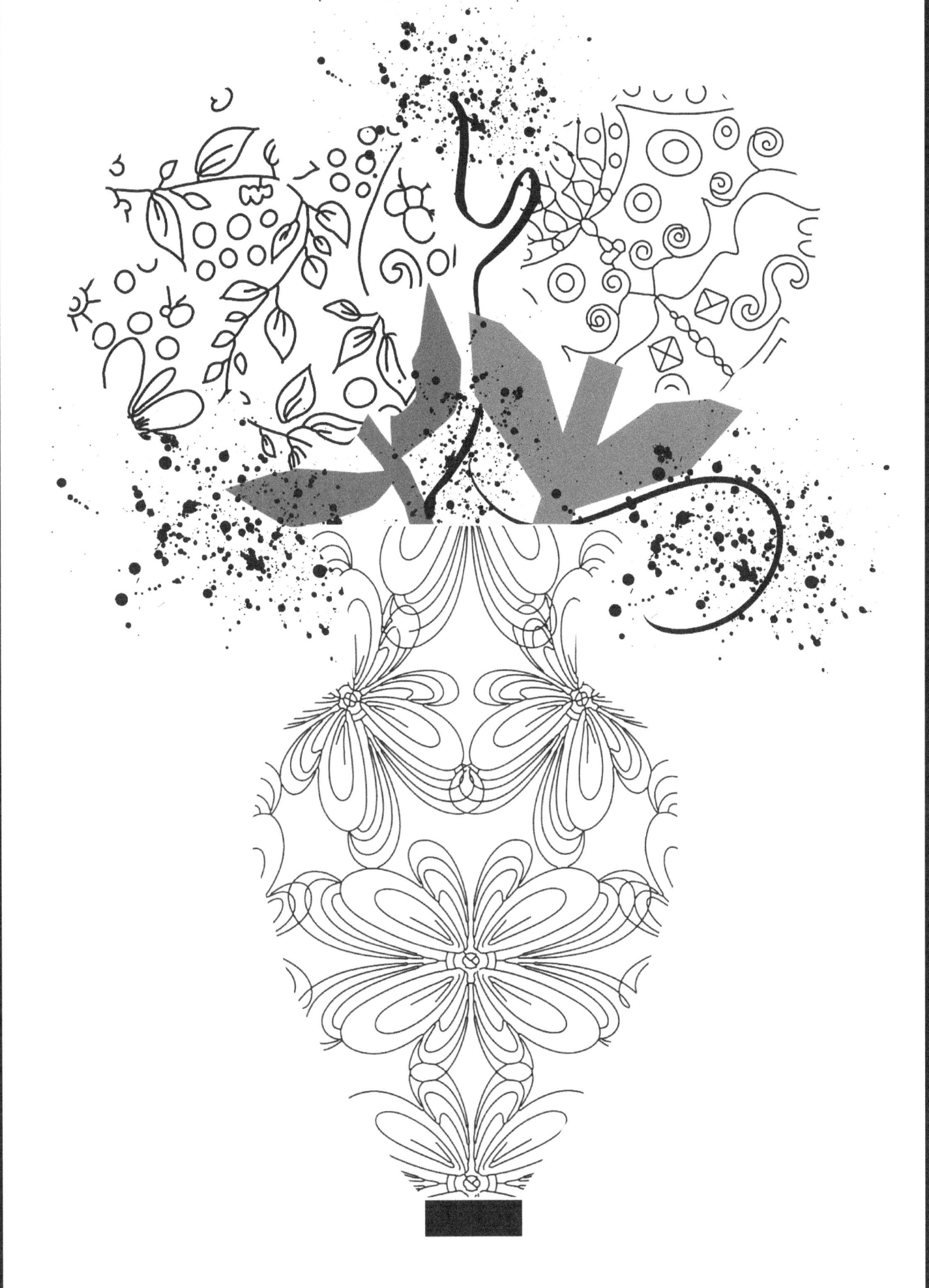

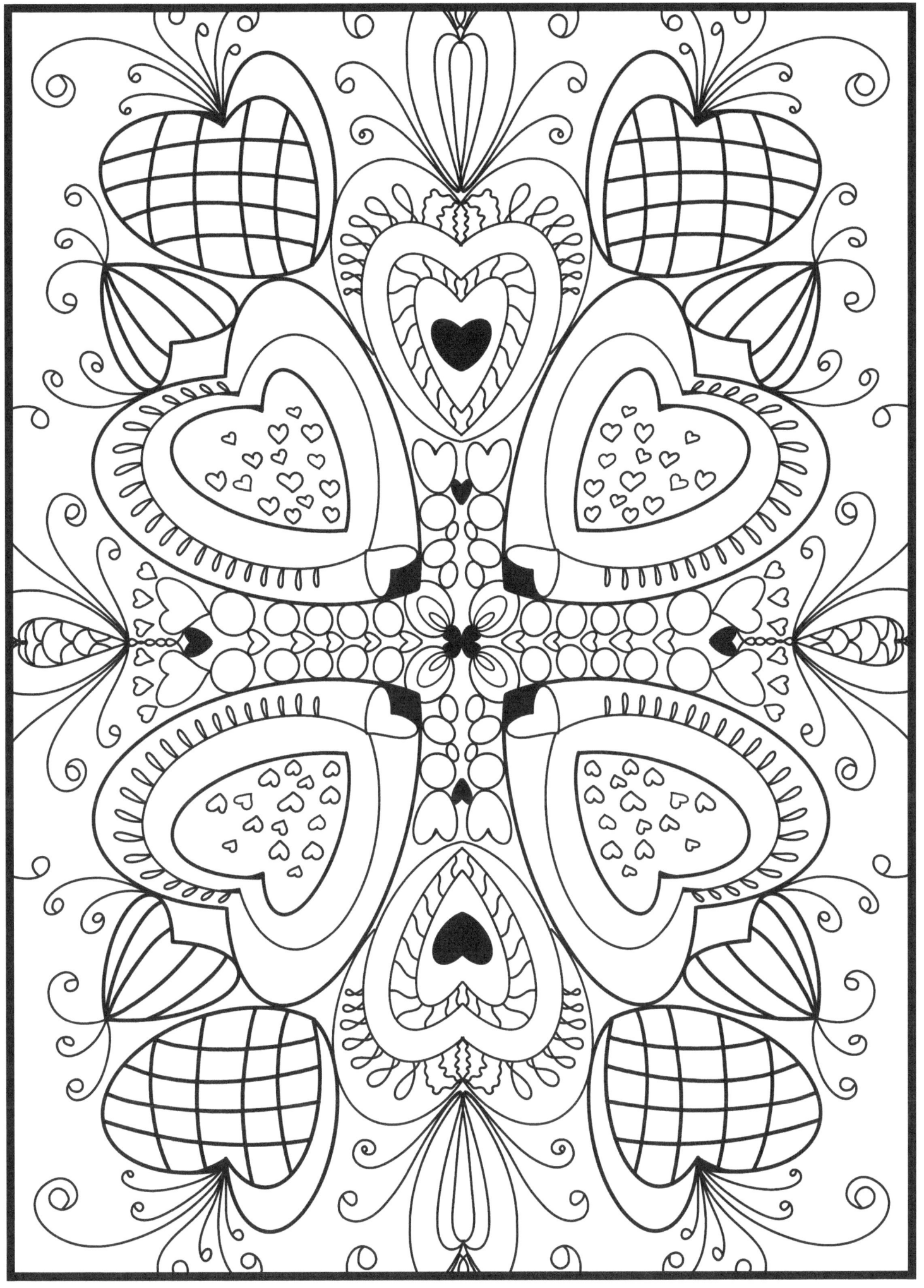

Hearts Galore

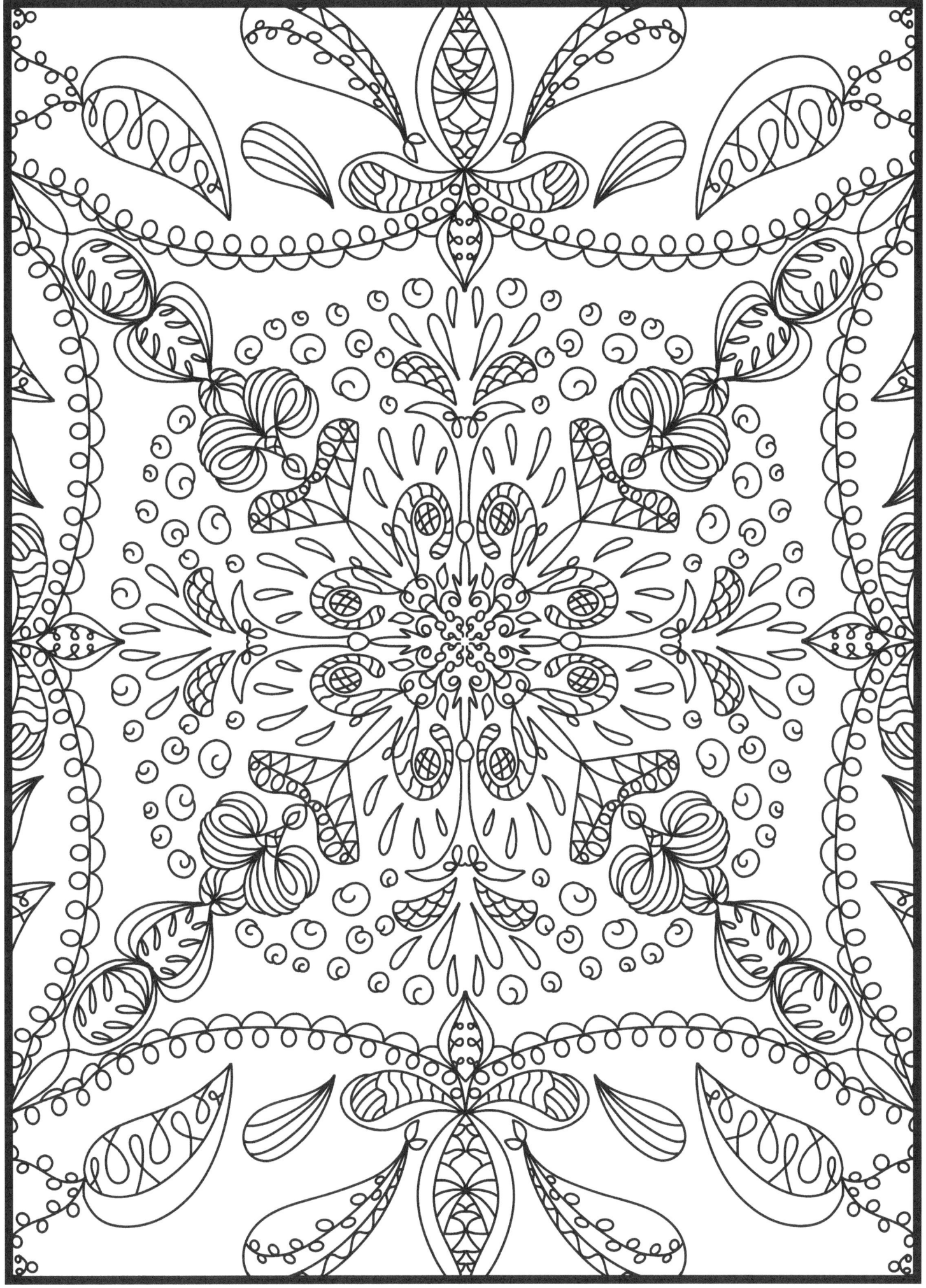

Blessings

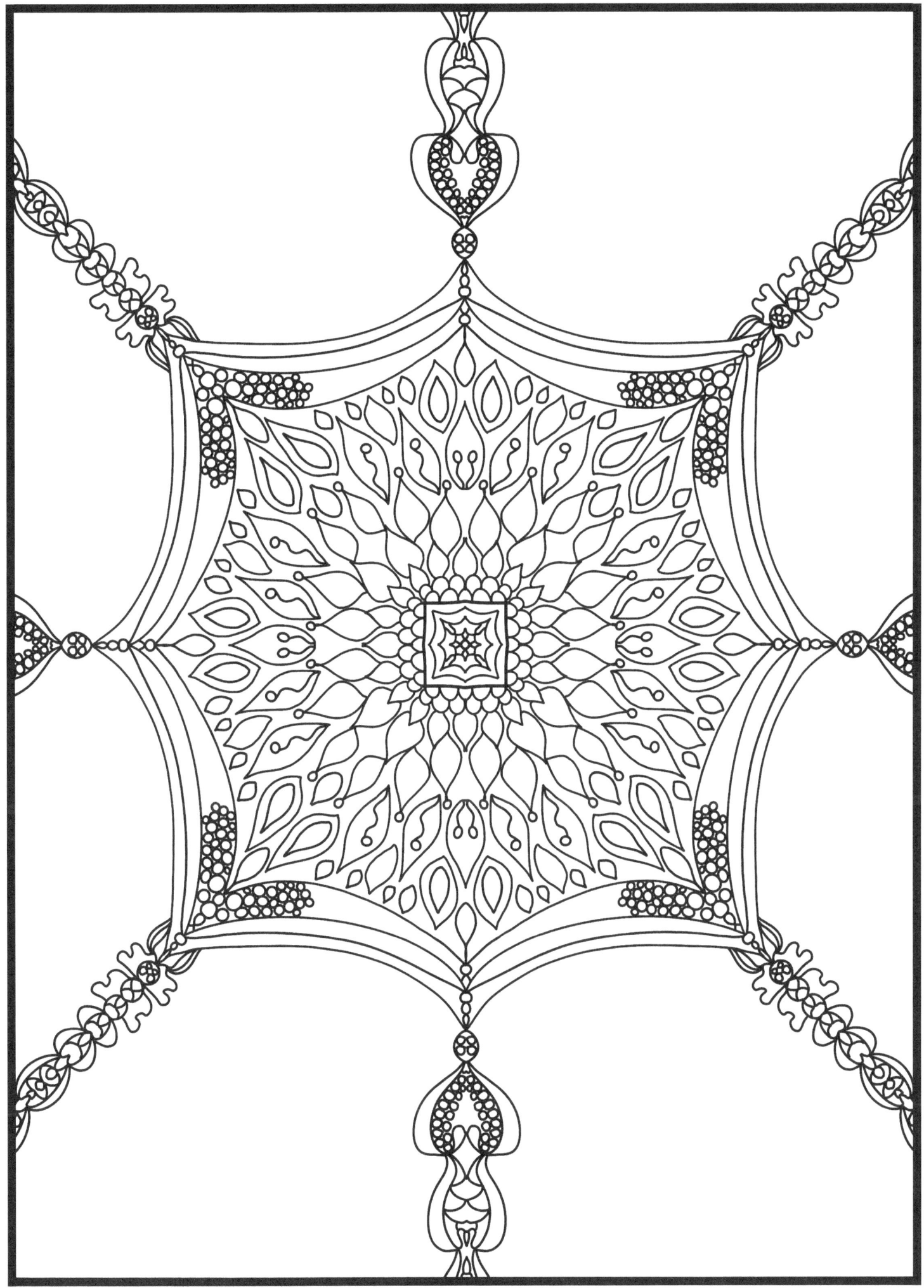

Life Focus

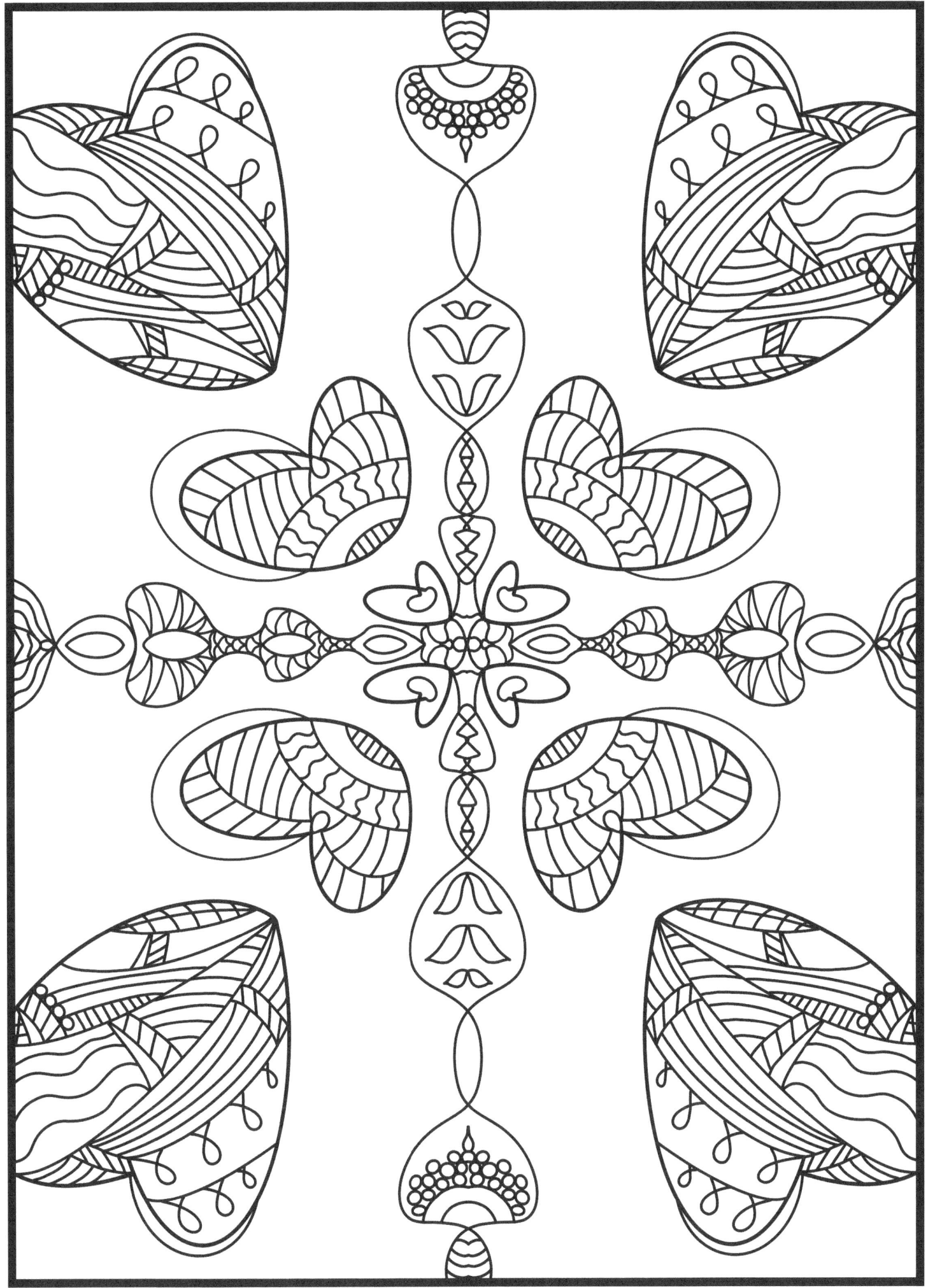

Fill in spaces

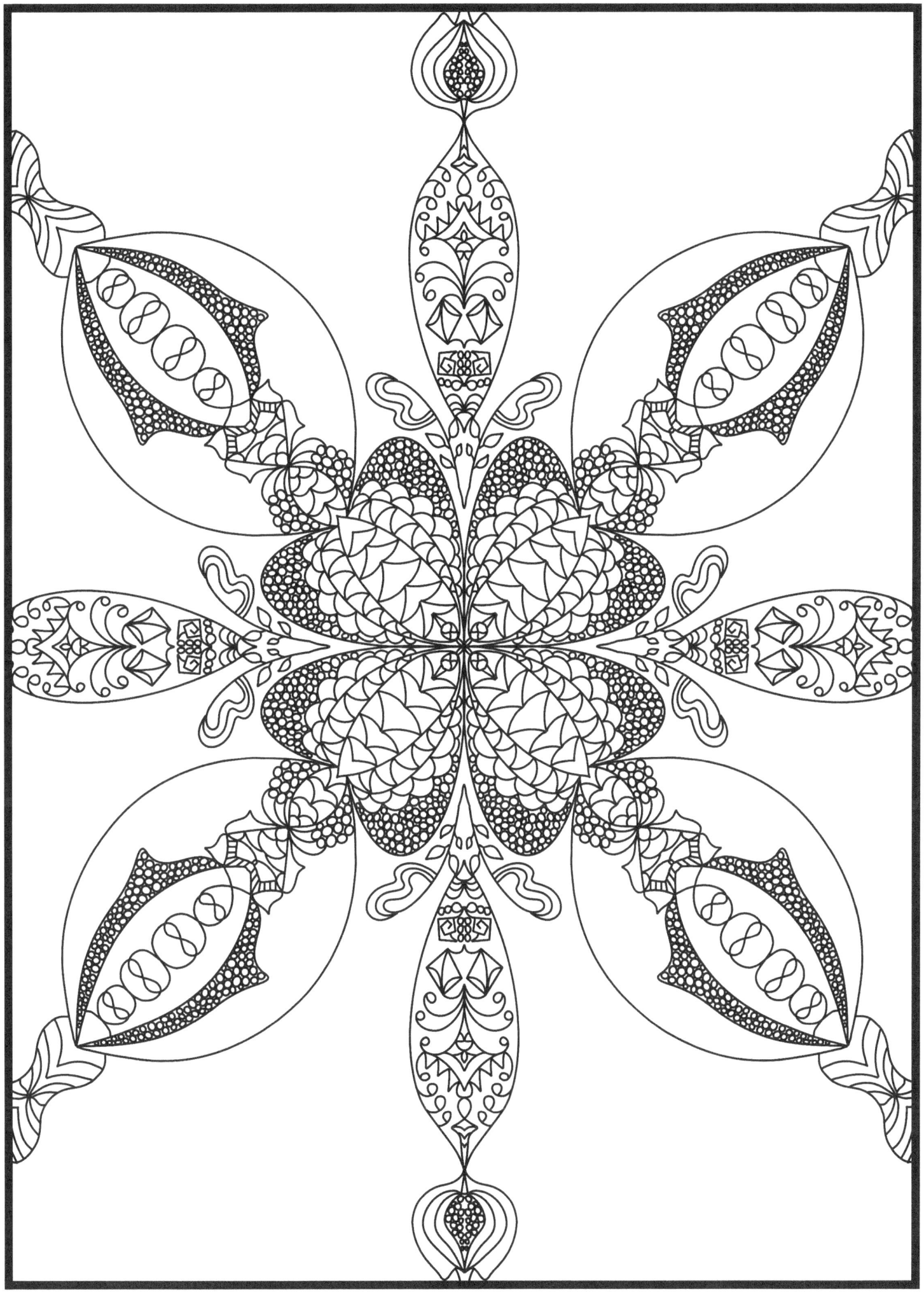

Find Joy

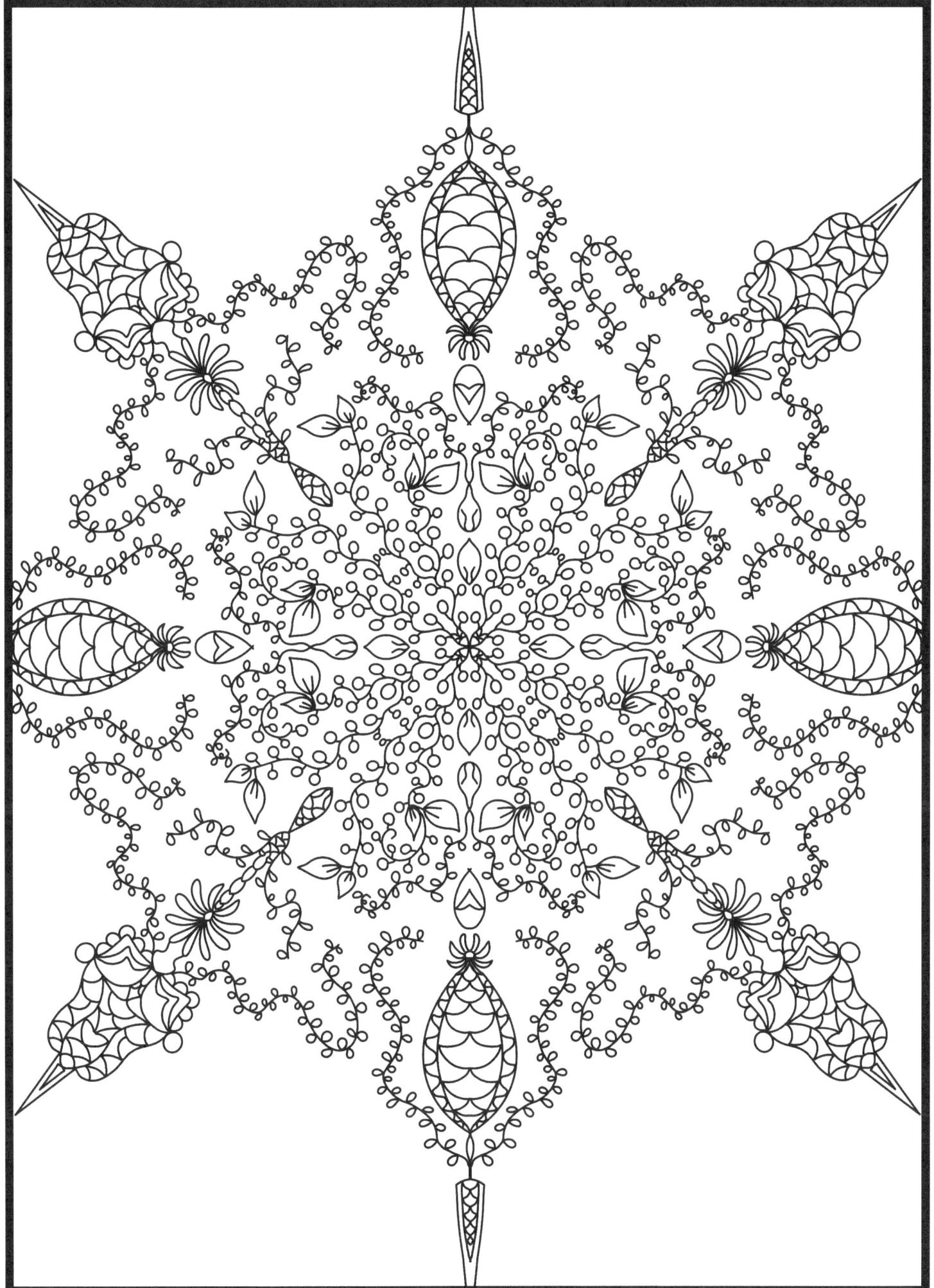

Pray

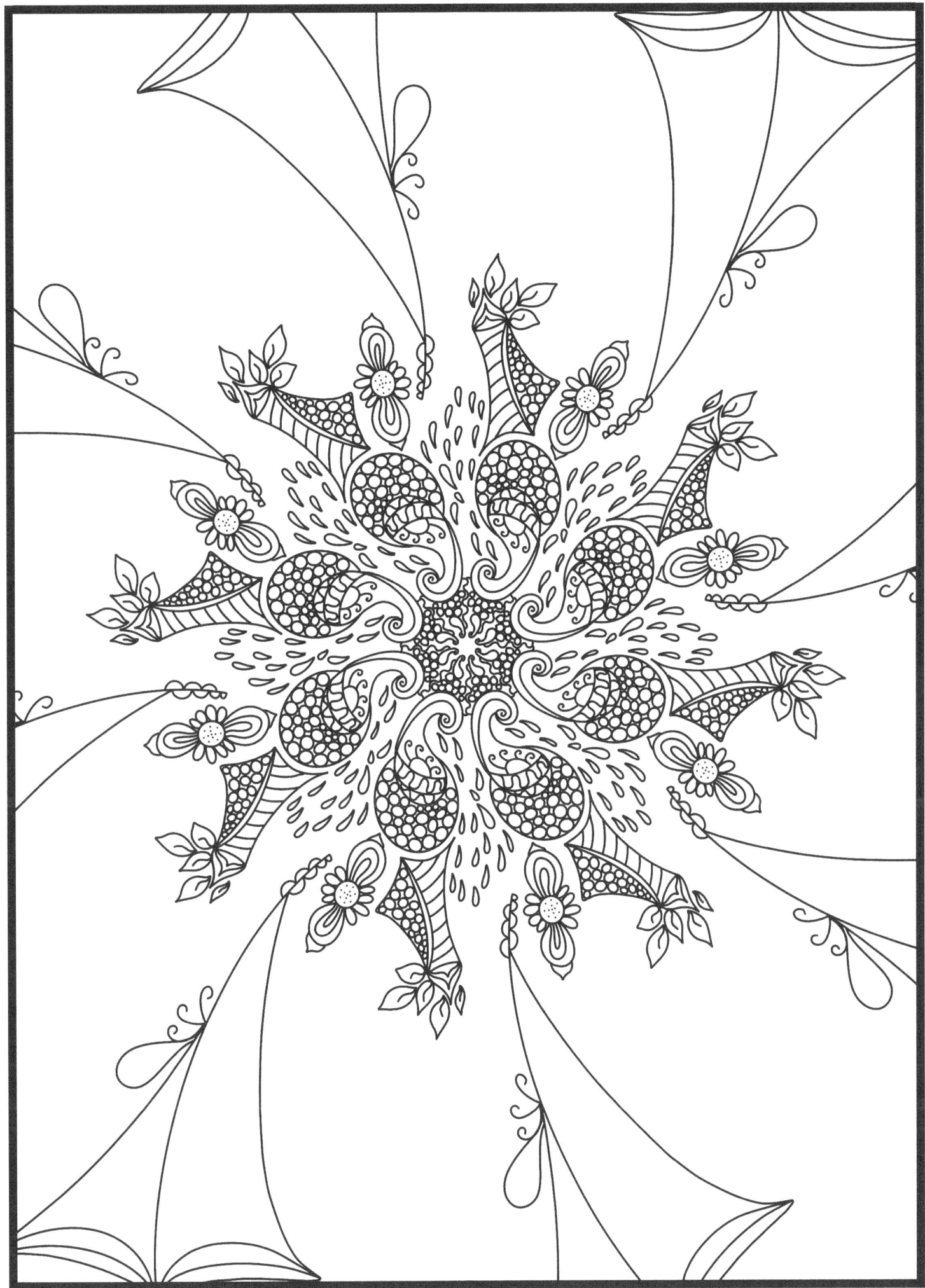

Add Design

~~~~~~~~~~~~~~~~~~~~~~

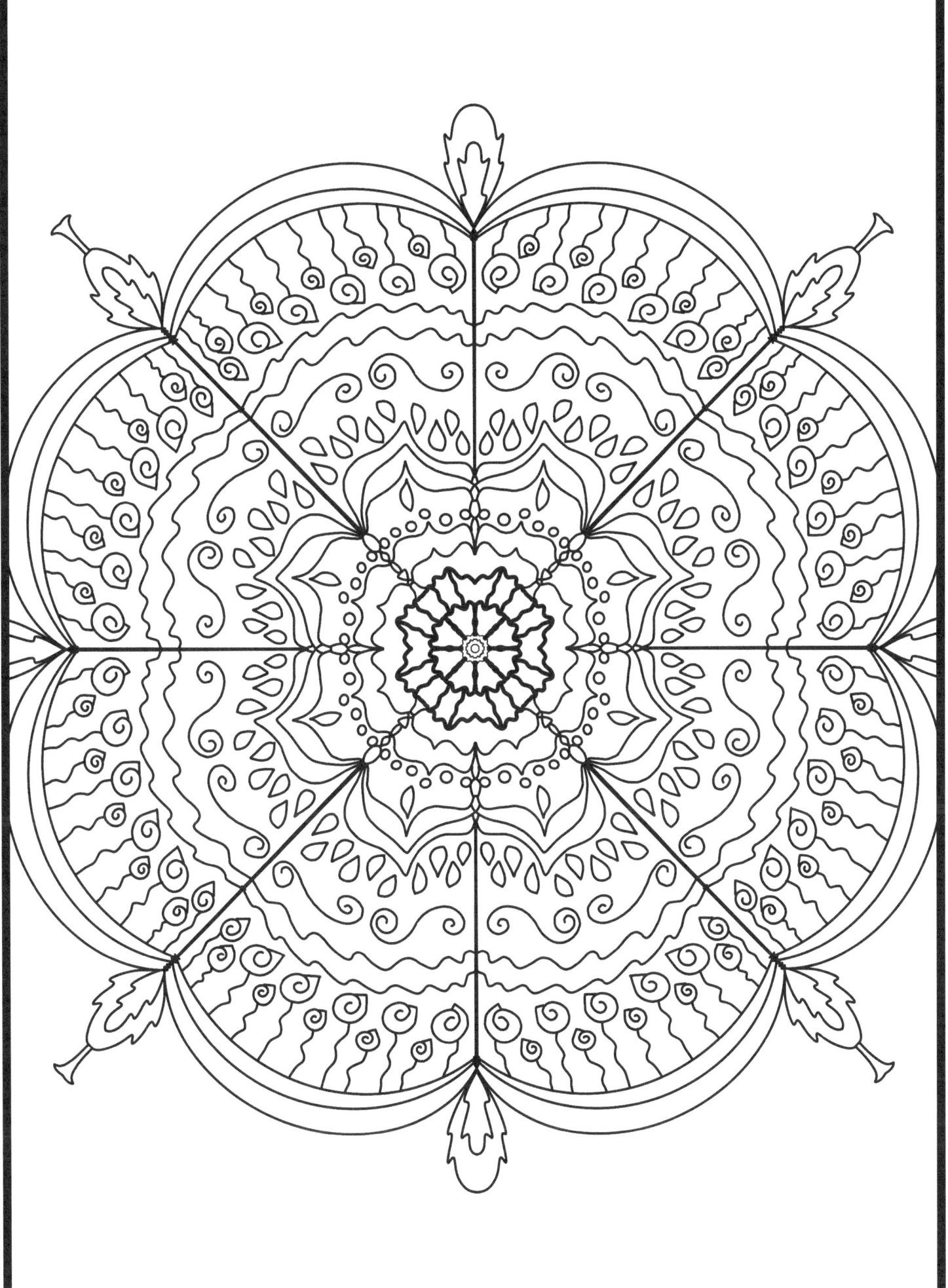

Garden Map

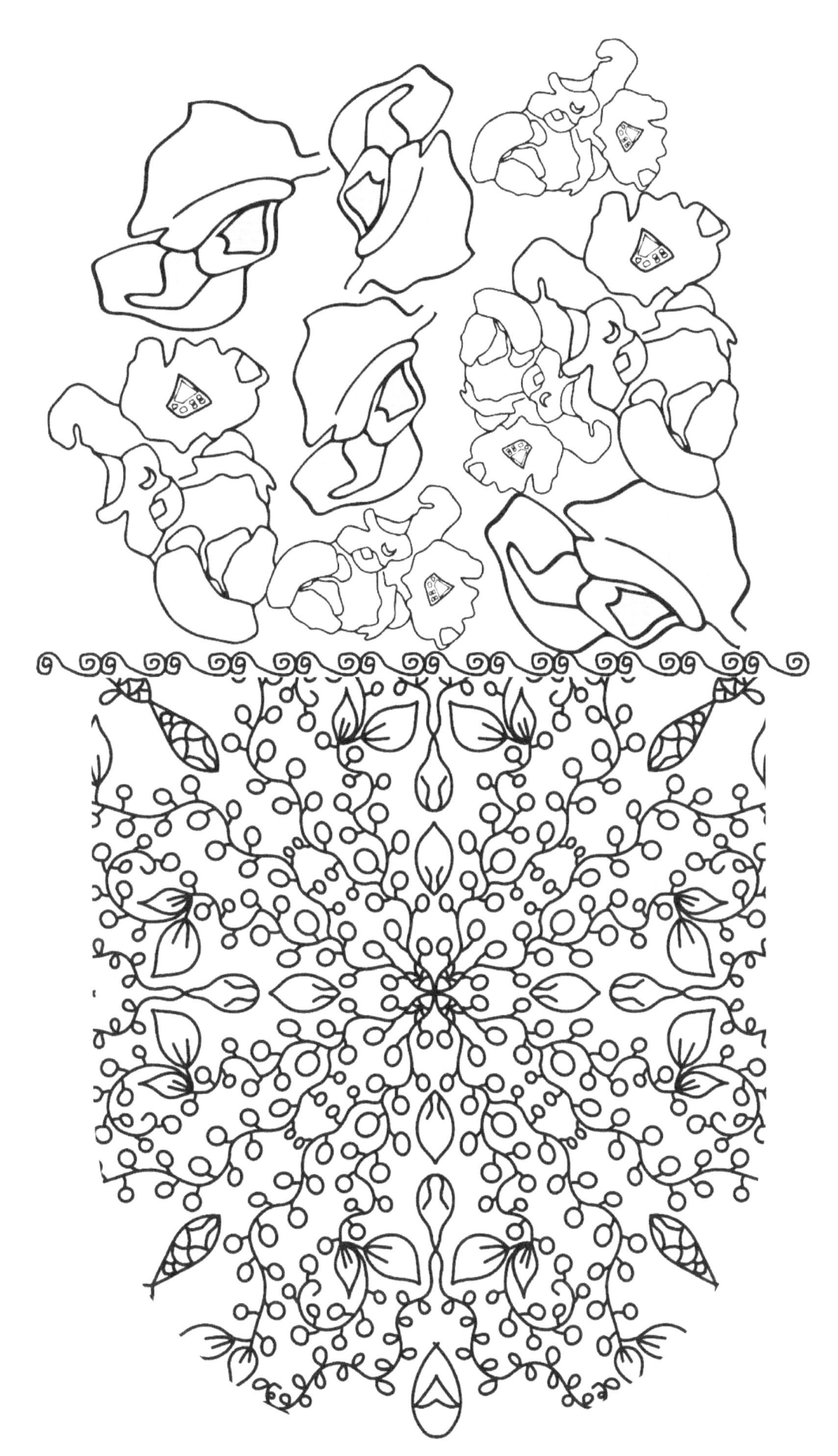

Bowl of Popcorn

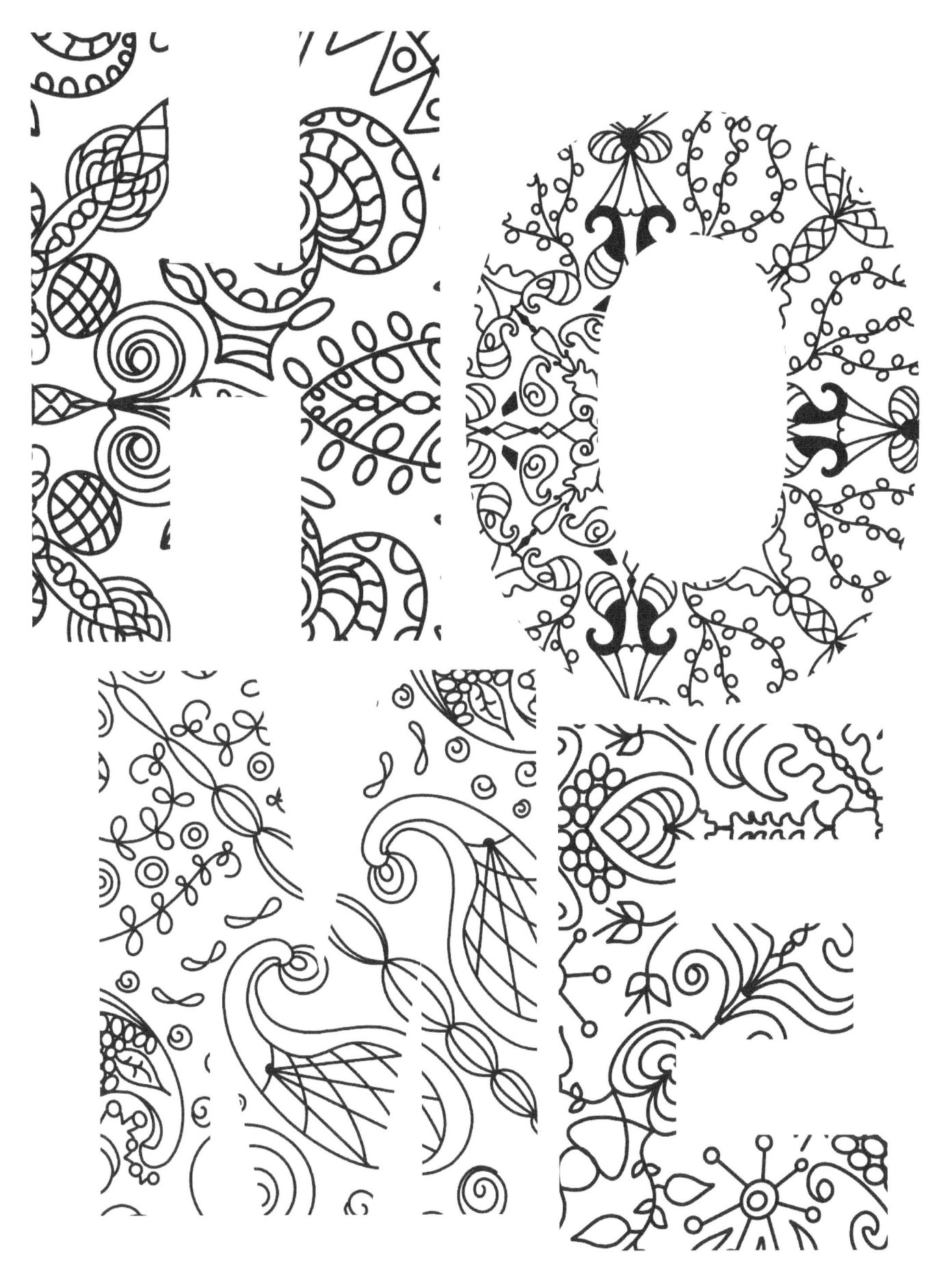

Home Sweet Home

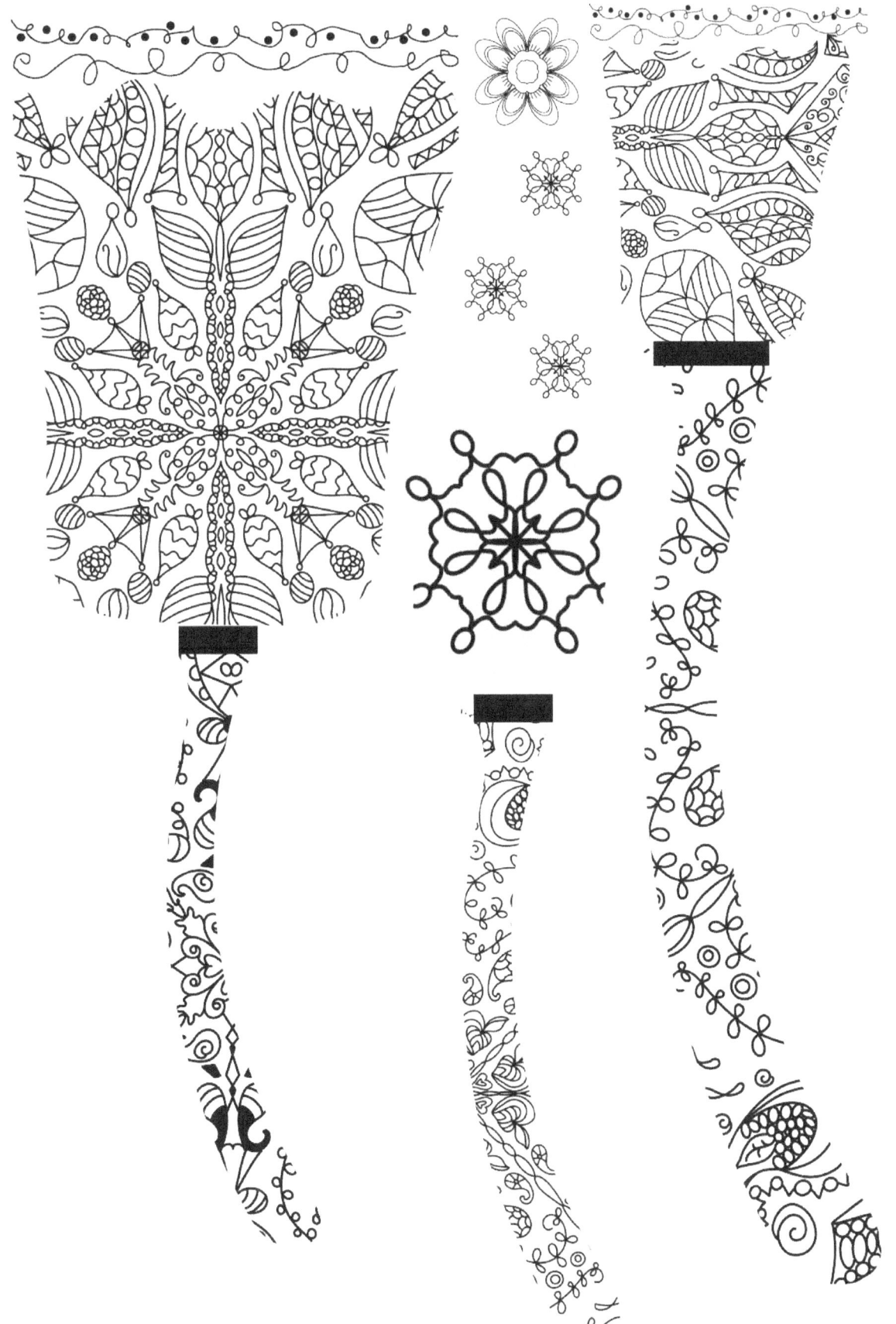

Tulips
~~~~~~~~~~~~~~~~~~~~~~

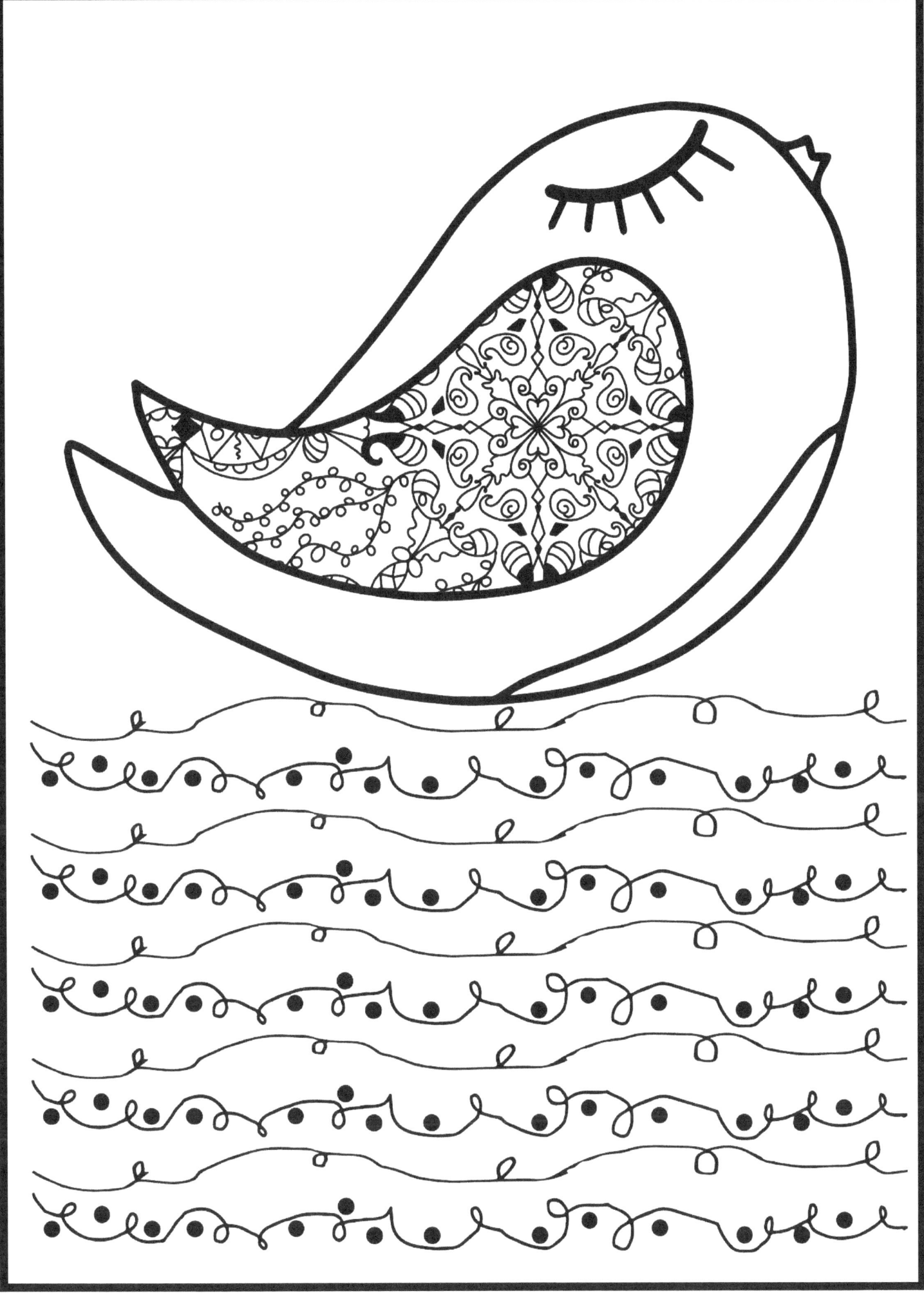

Birdie

Butterflies

White Snowflake

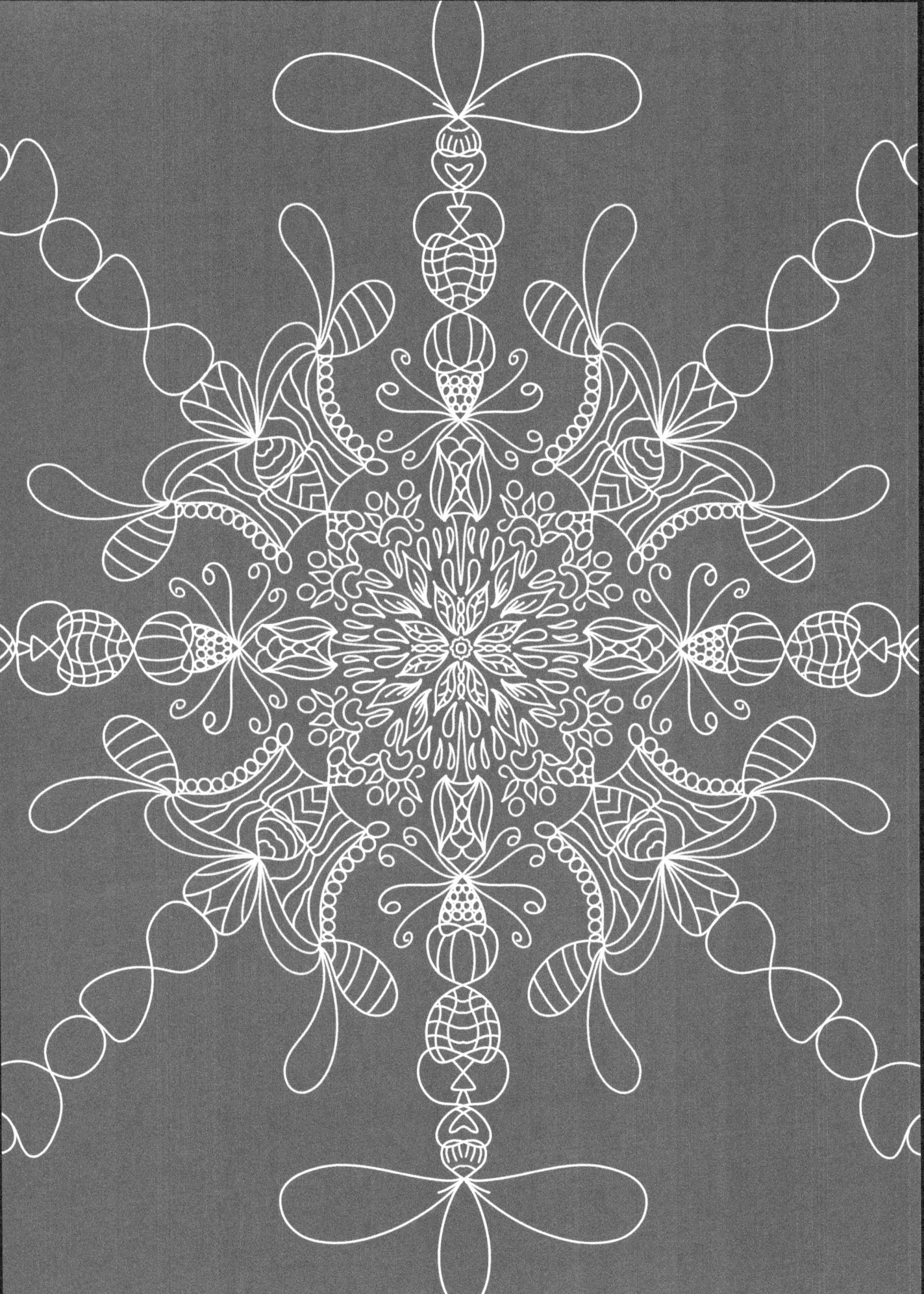

Evening Coloring

Try Neon Coloring

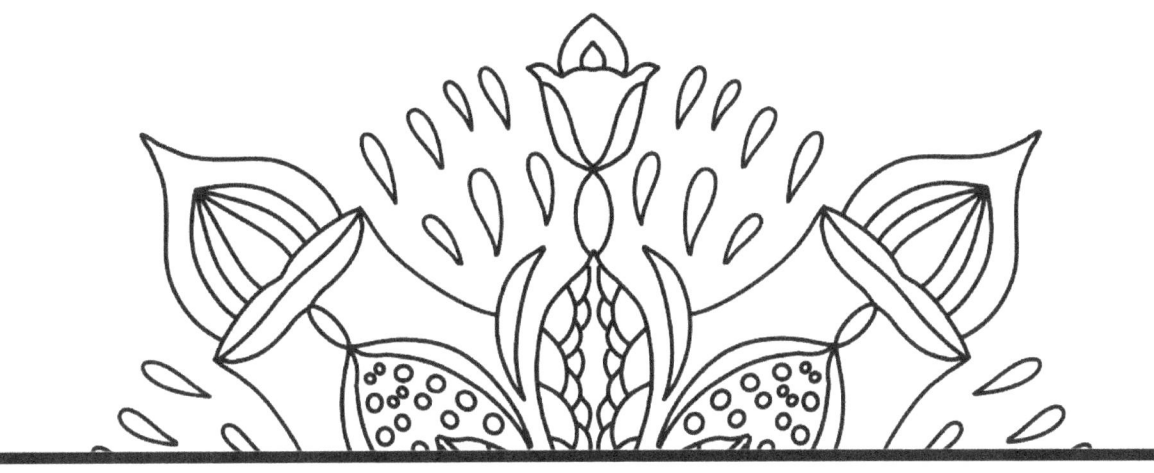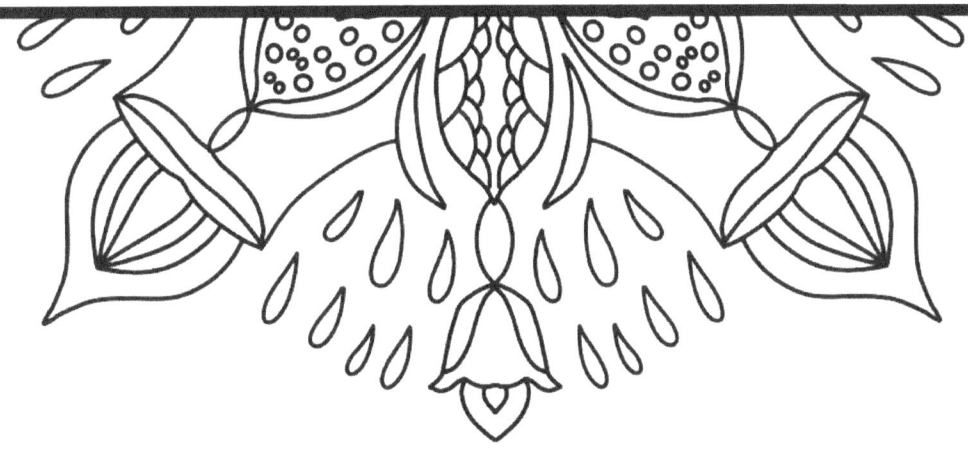

Family Crest

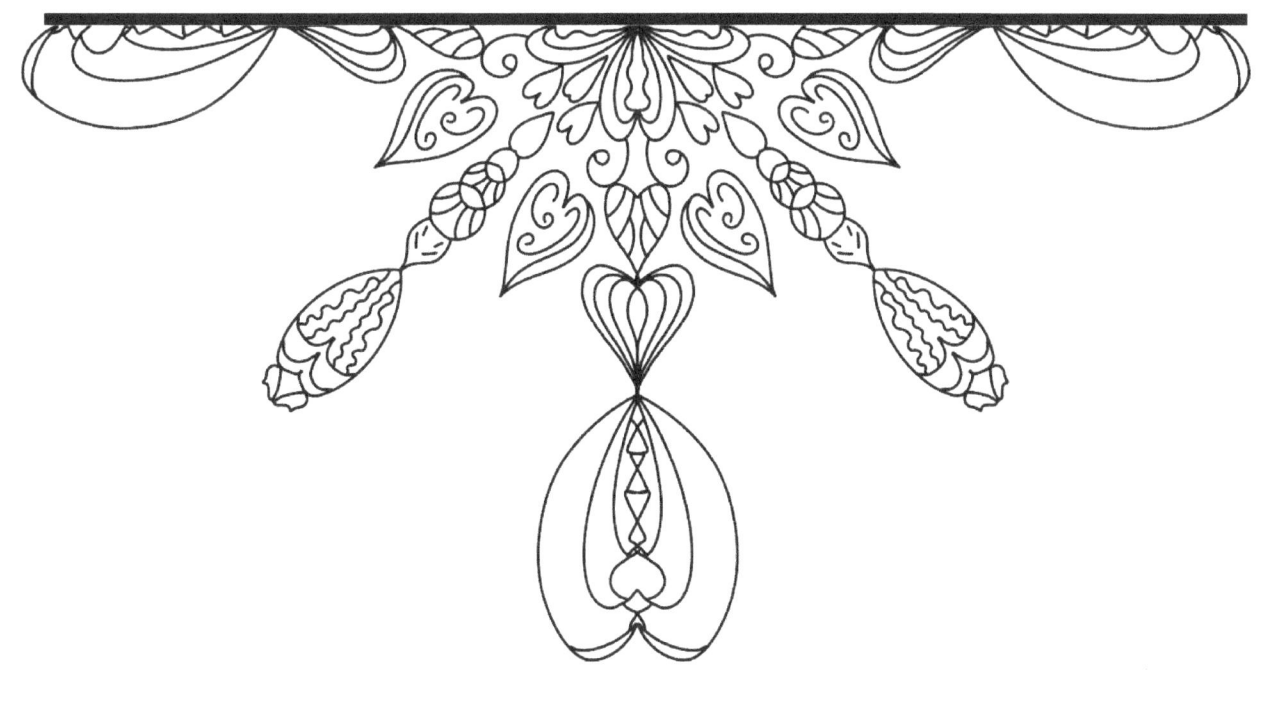

Welcome Sign

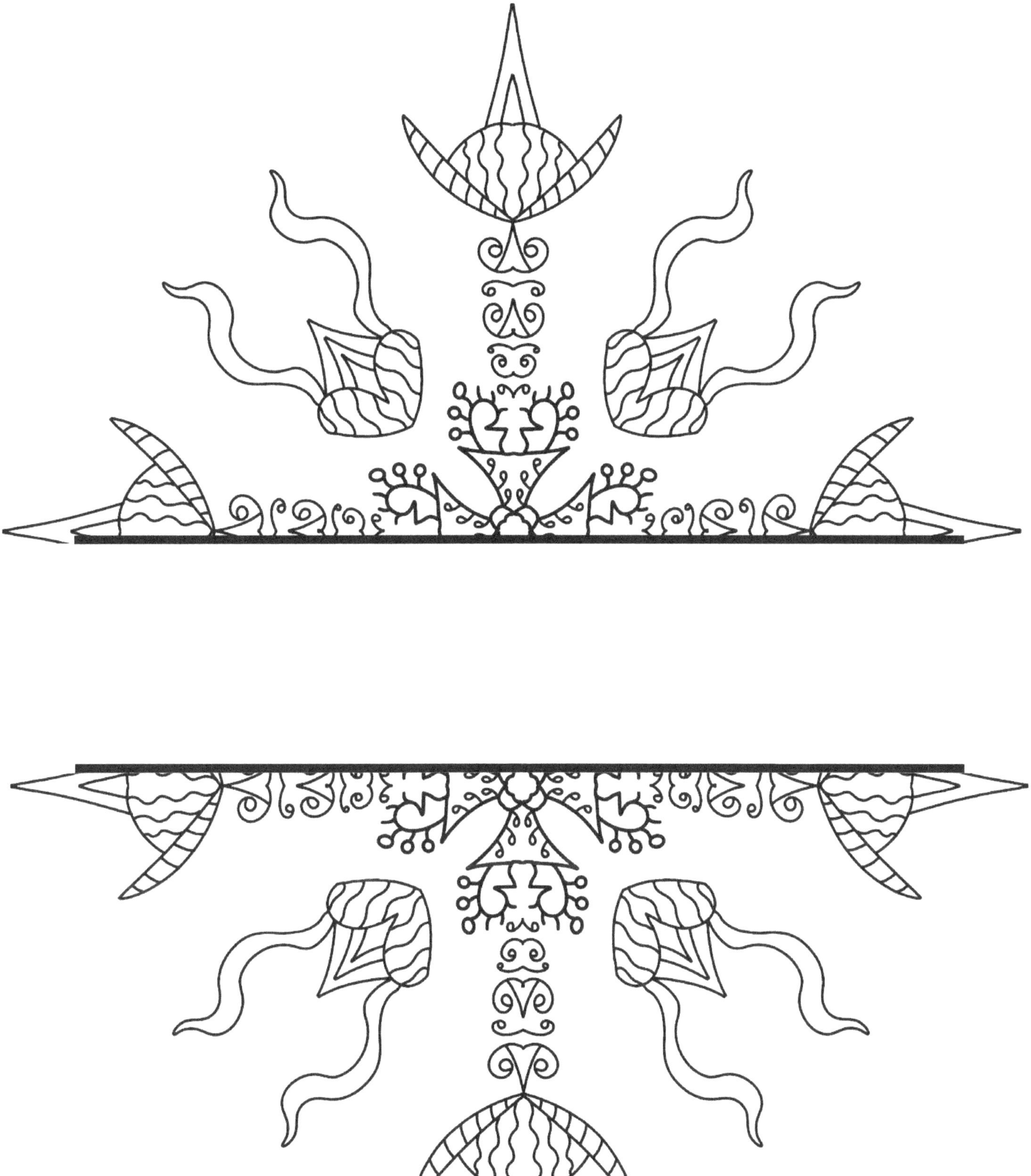

Guest Password

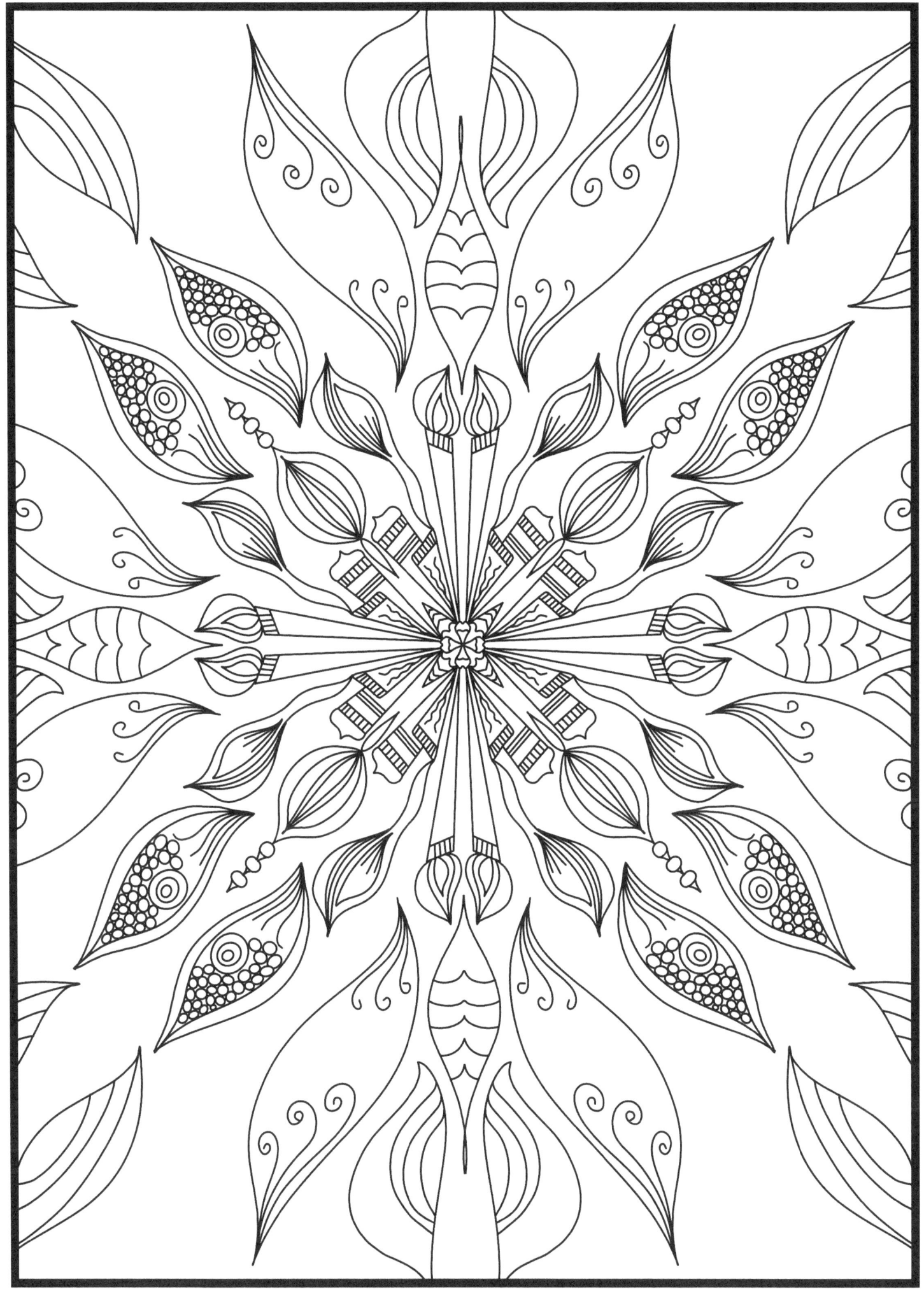

Comfort Foods

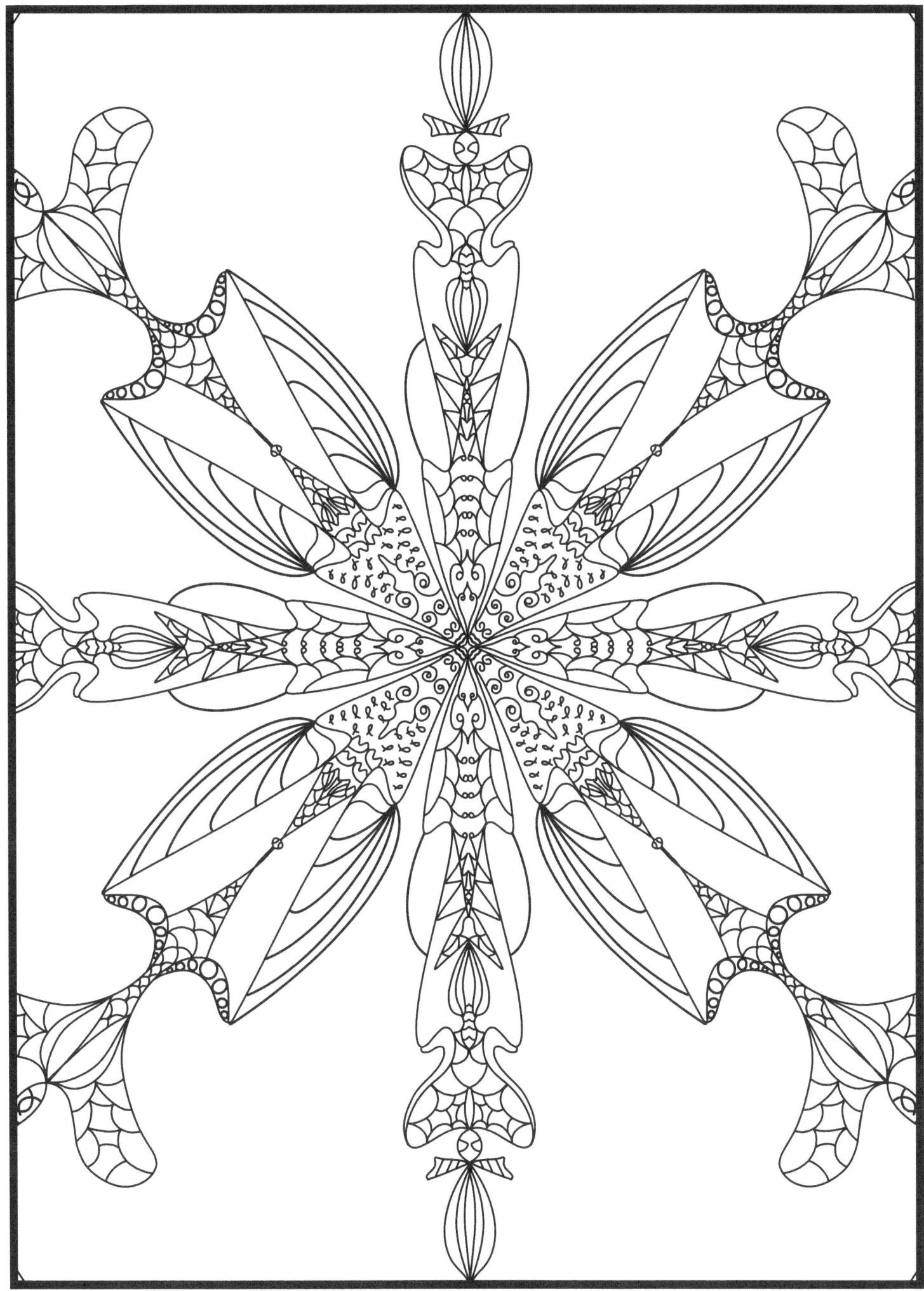

Fire Place

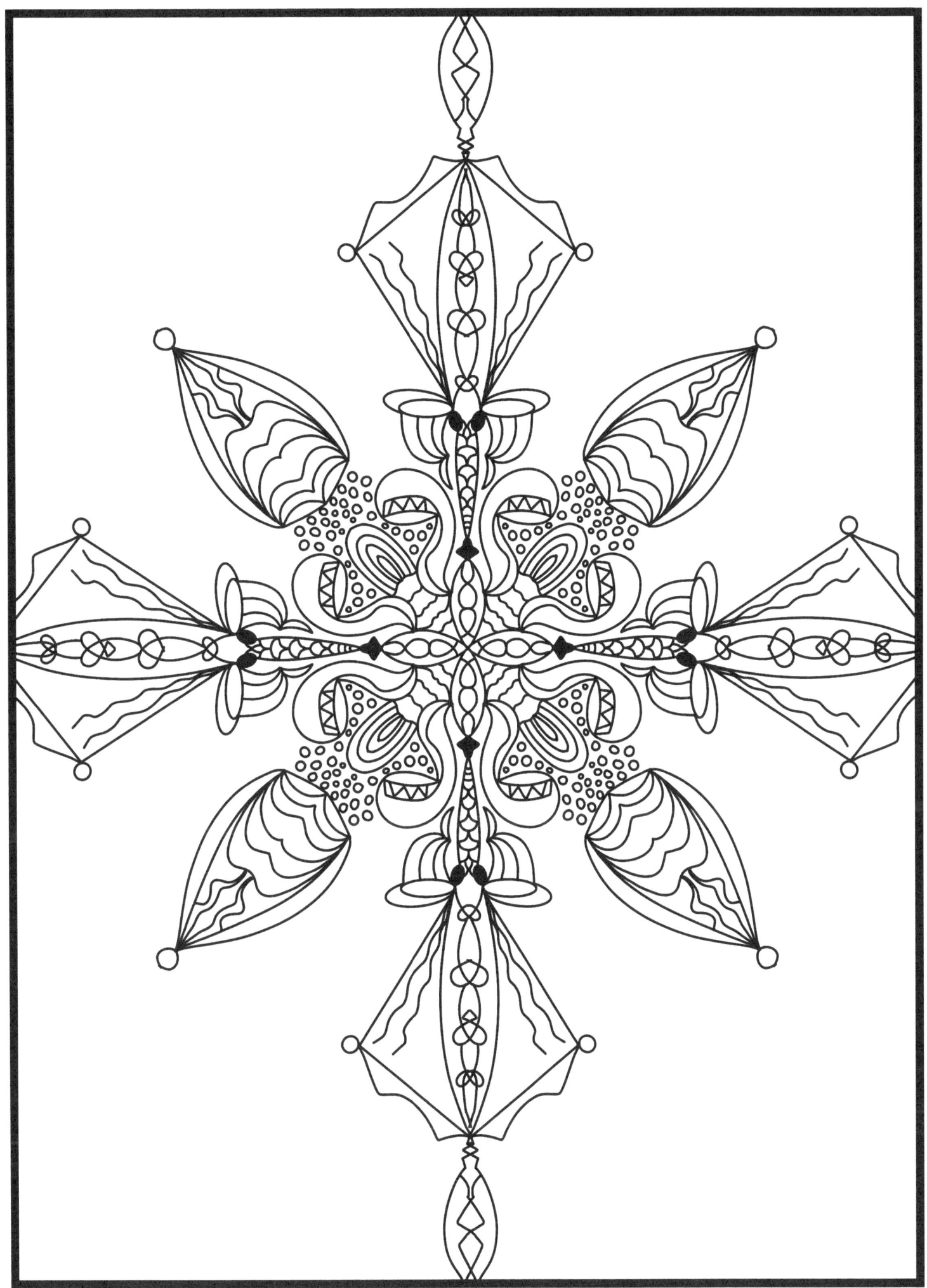

Lavender

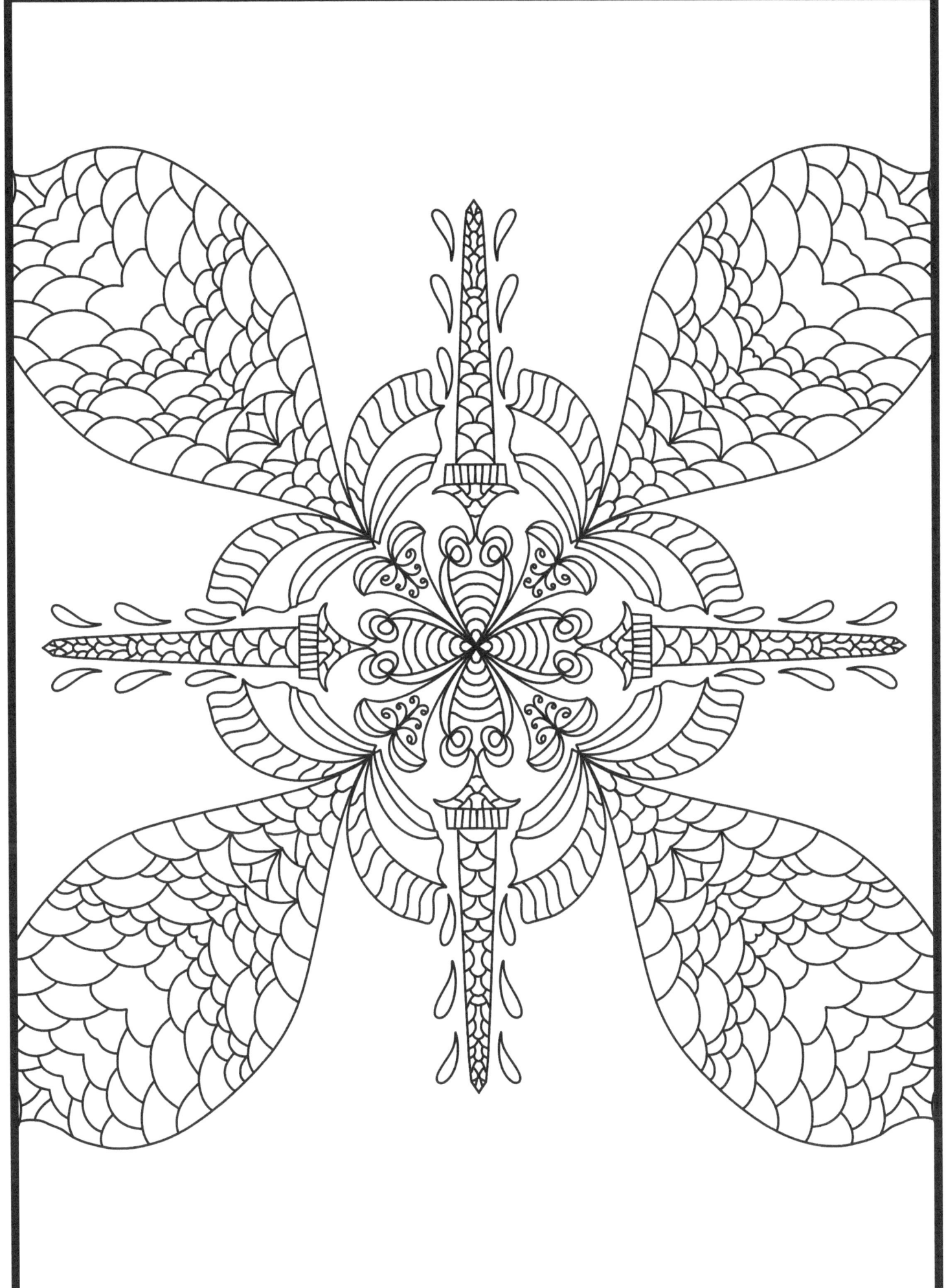

Herb Garden

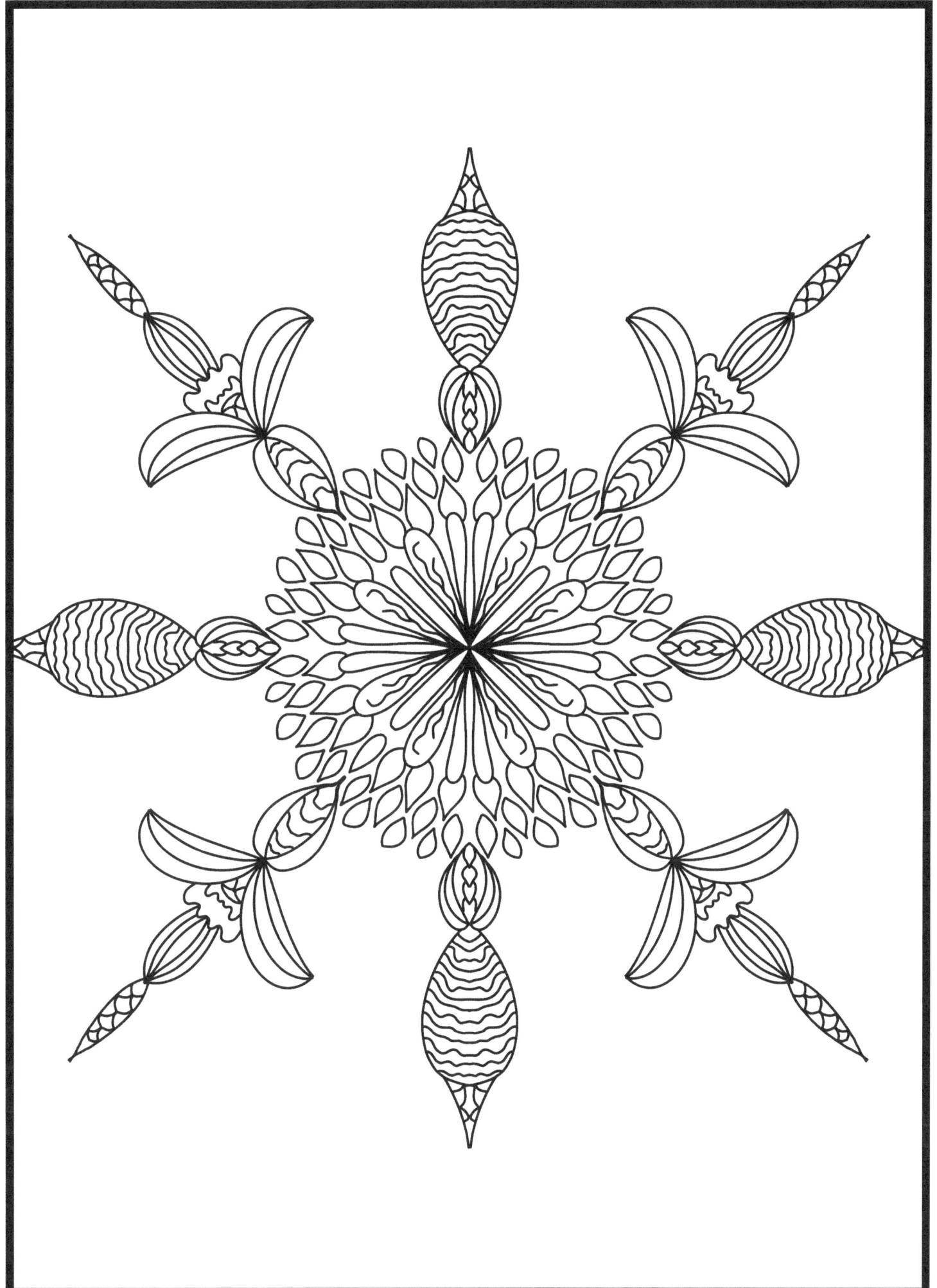

Peaceful Night

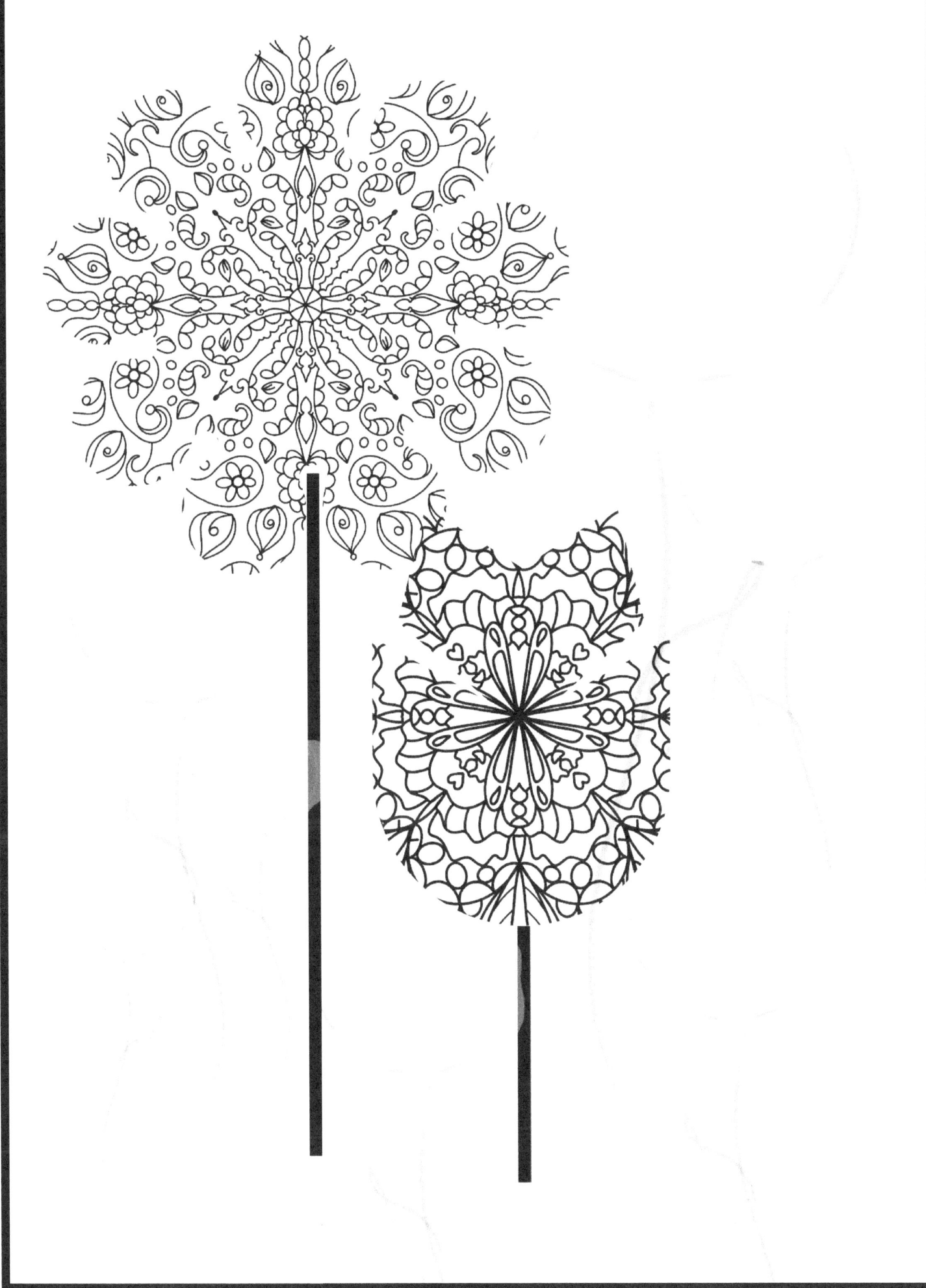

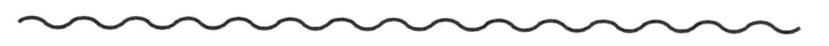

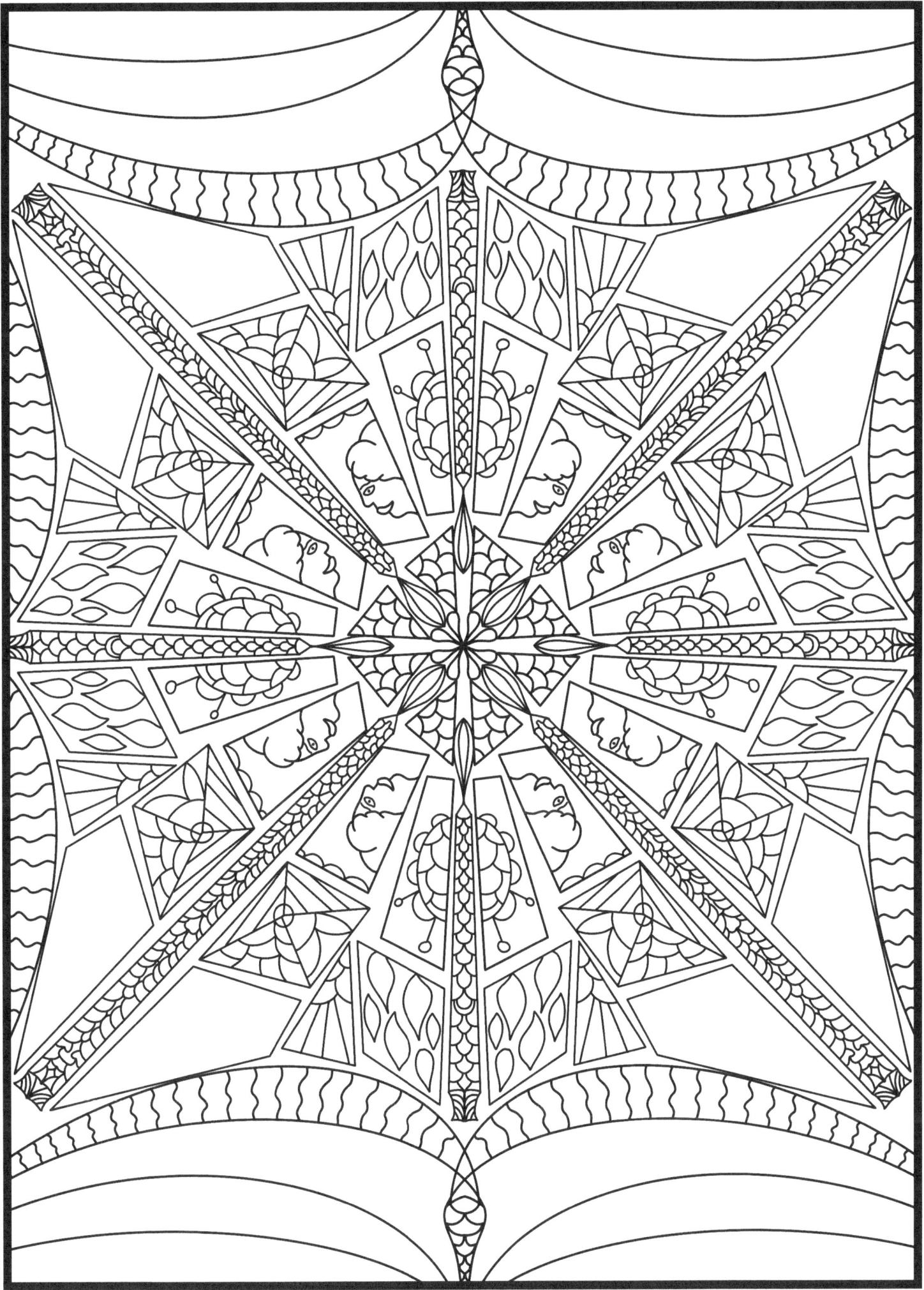

Stain Glass Beauty

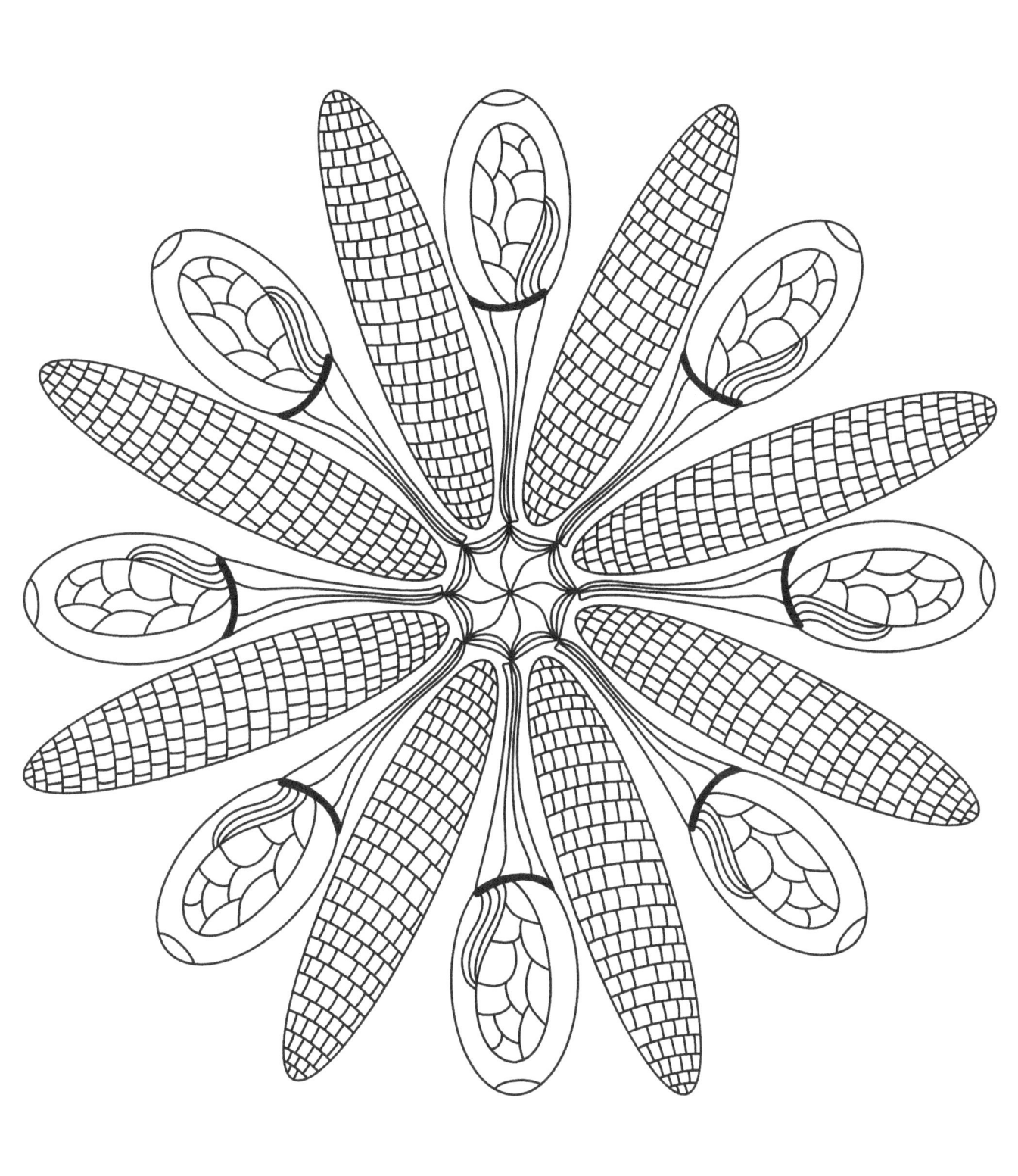

Fresh Air

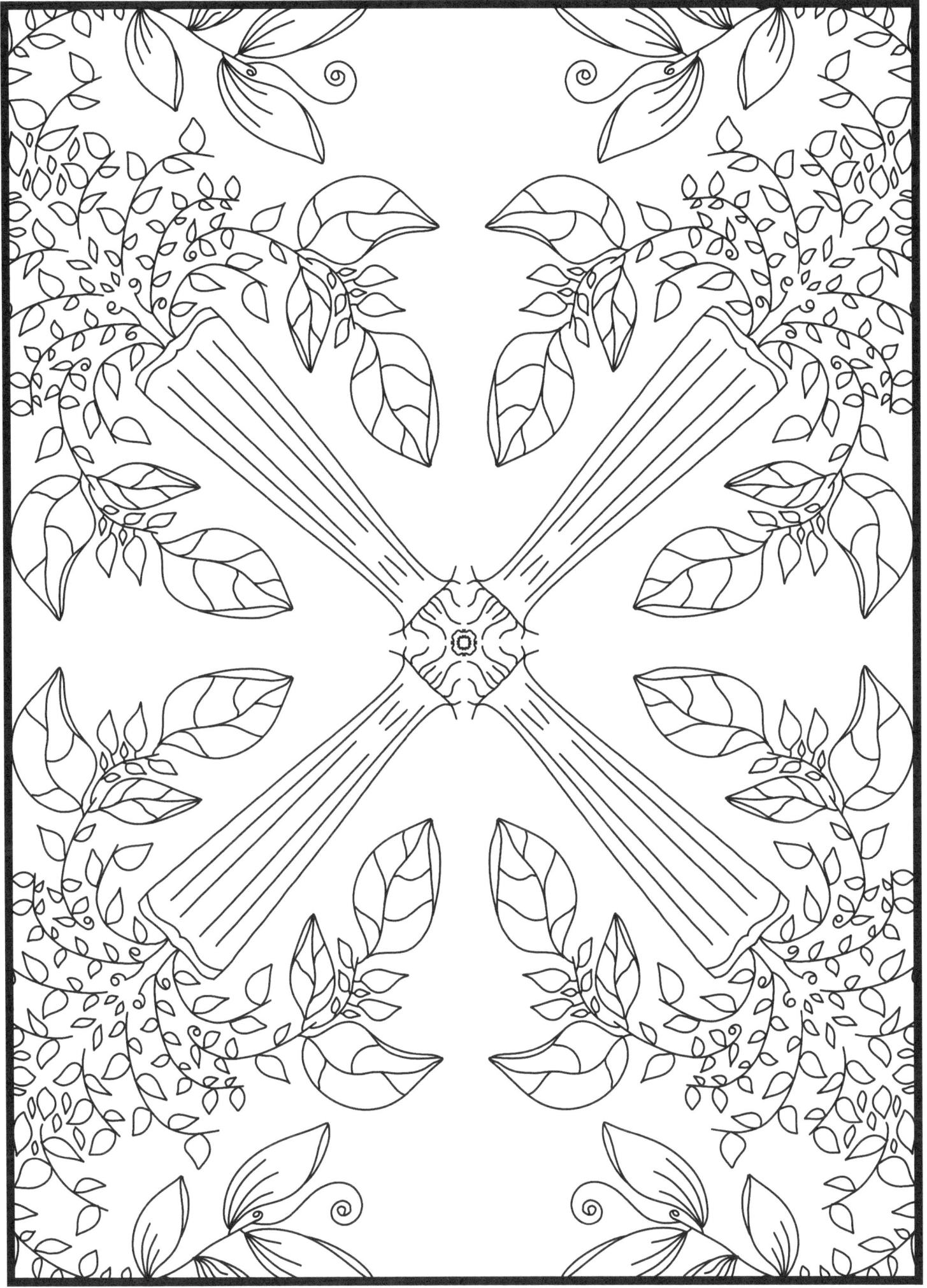

Trees
~~~~~~~~~~~~~~~~~~~~~~

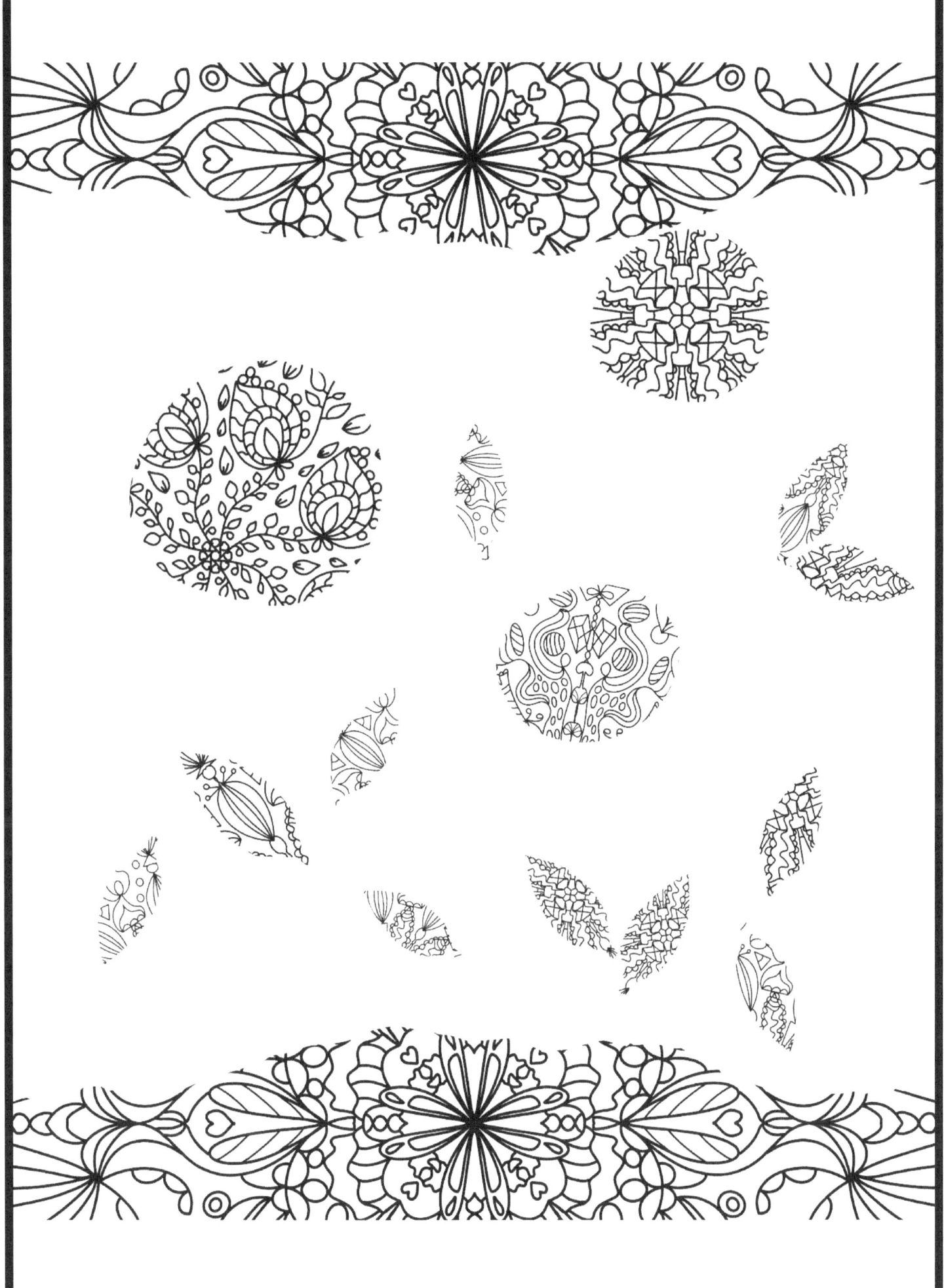

Sun Flowers

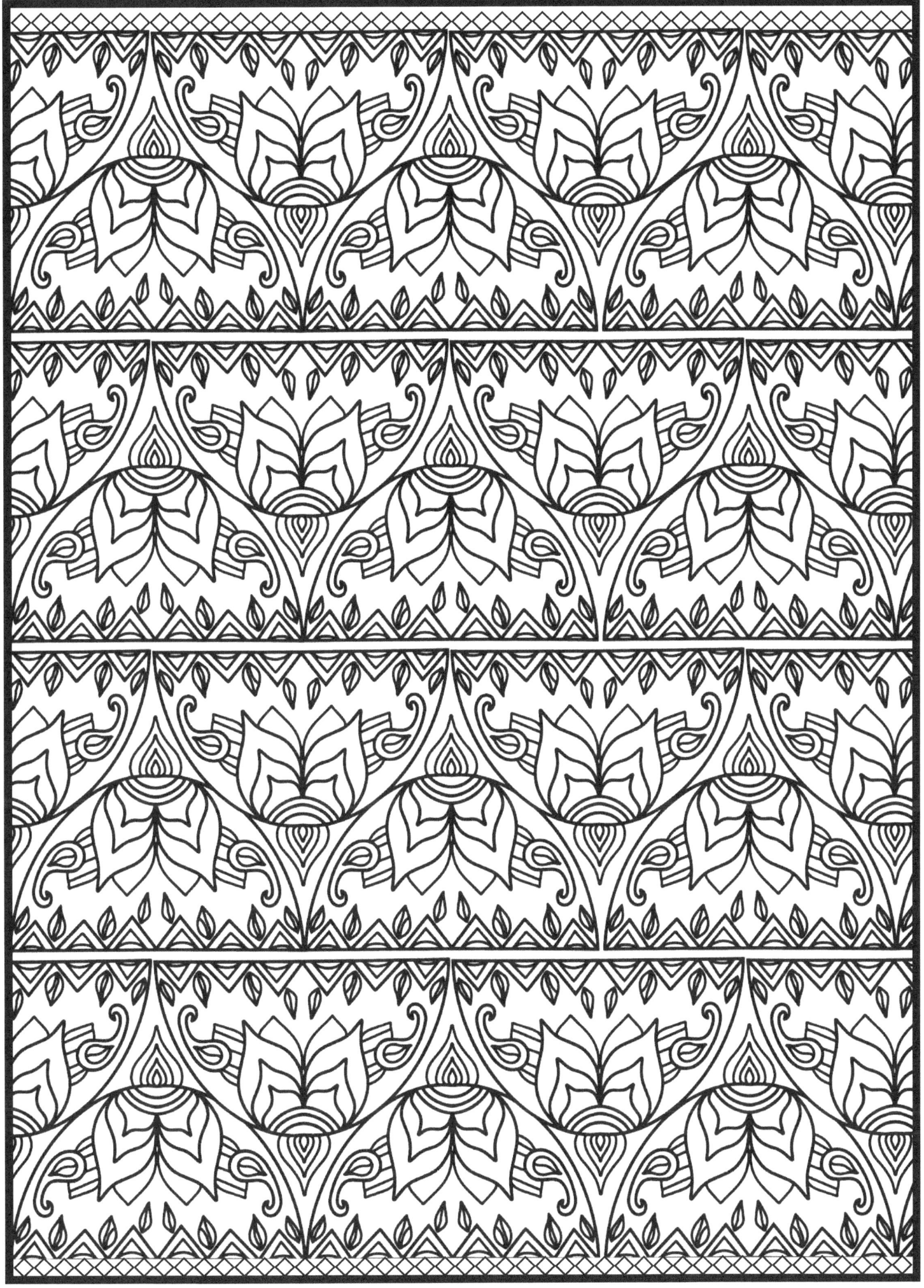

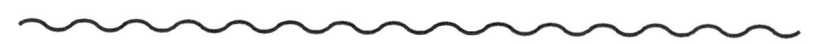

Peaceful Hopes

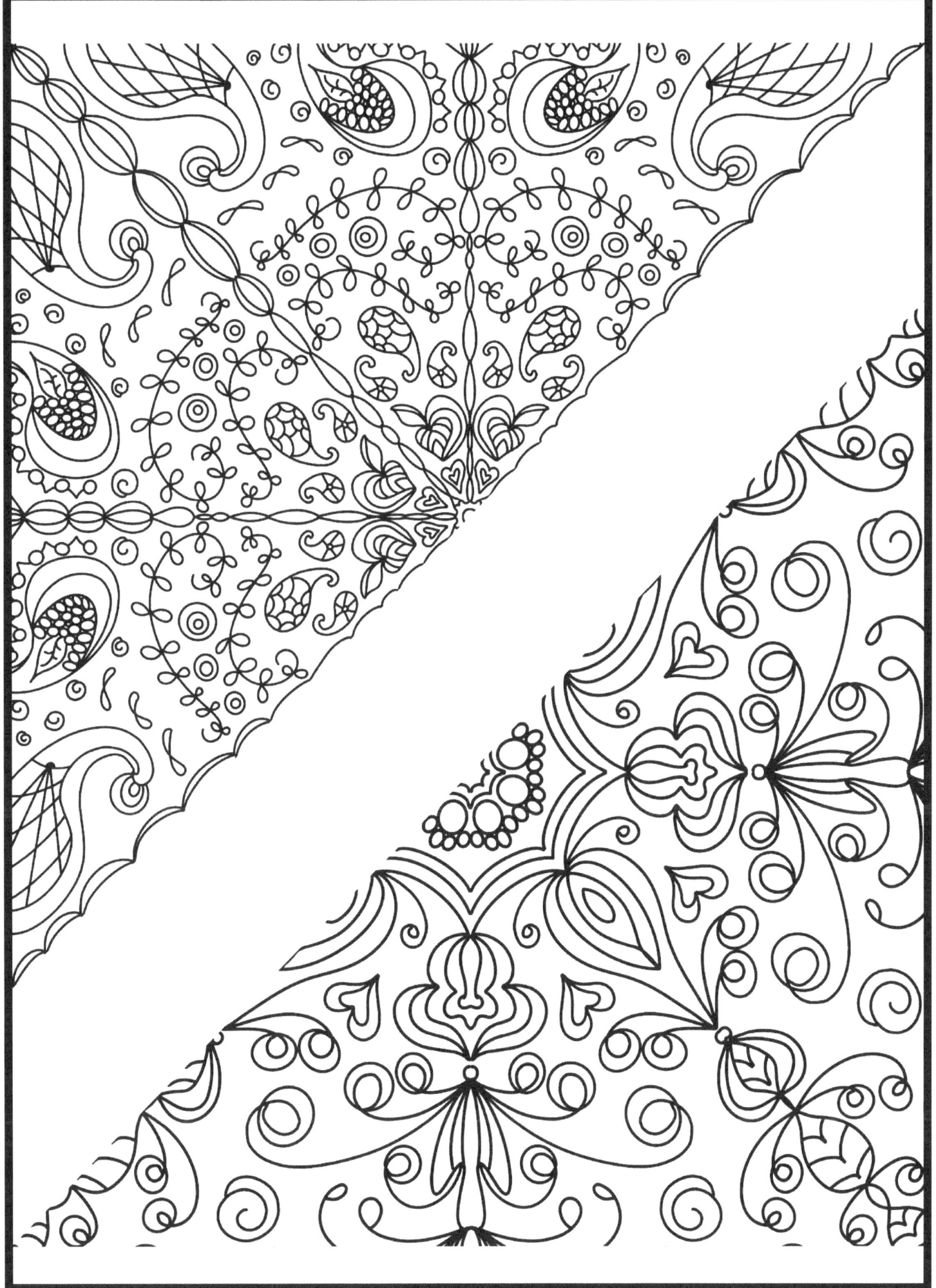

Unite Patterns

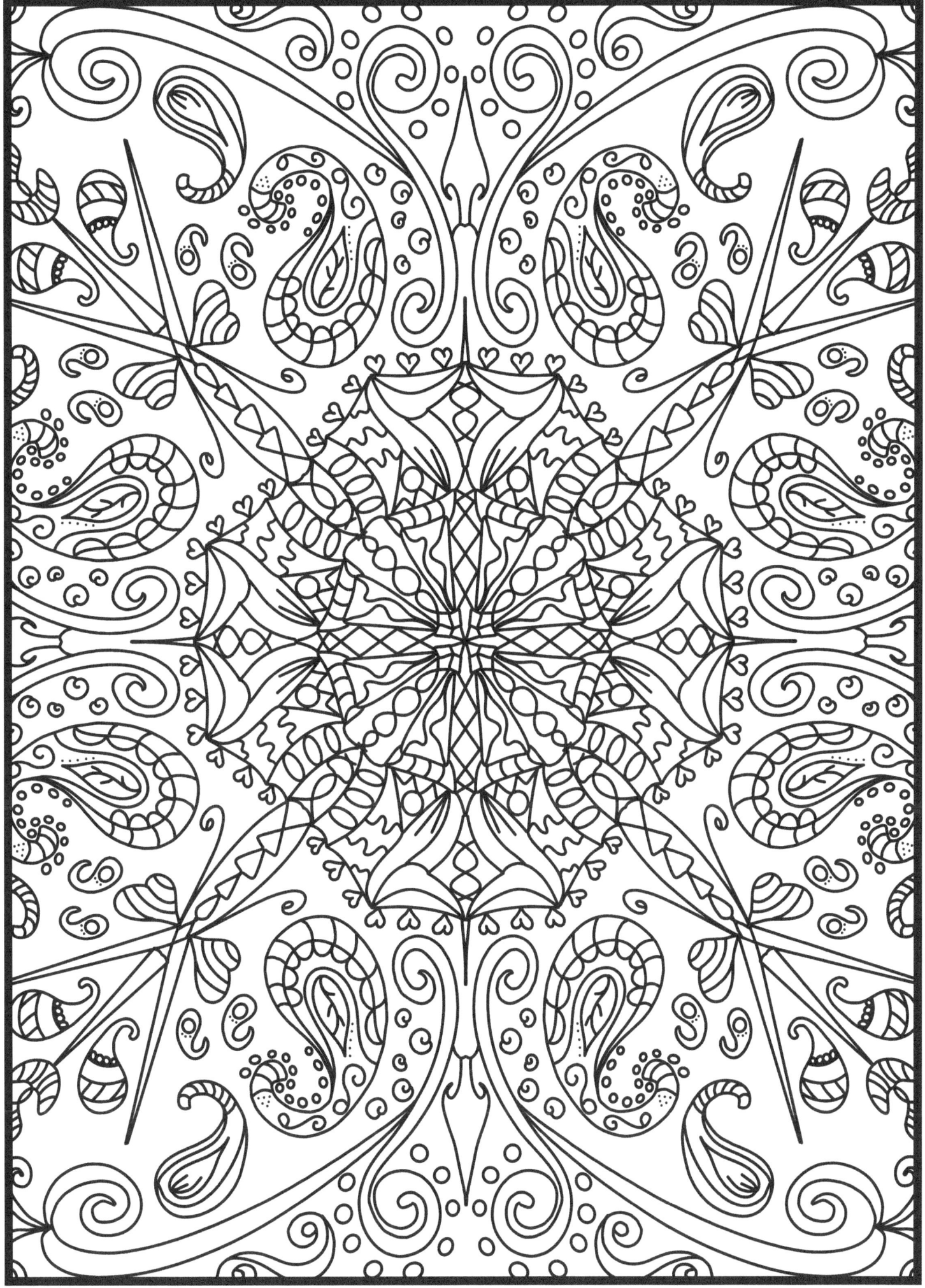

Peace Time

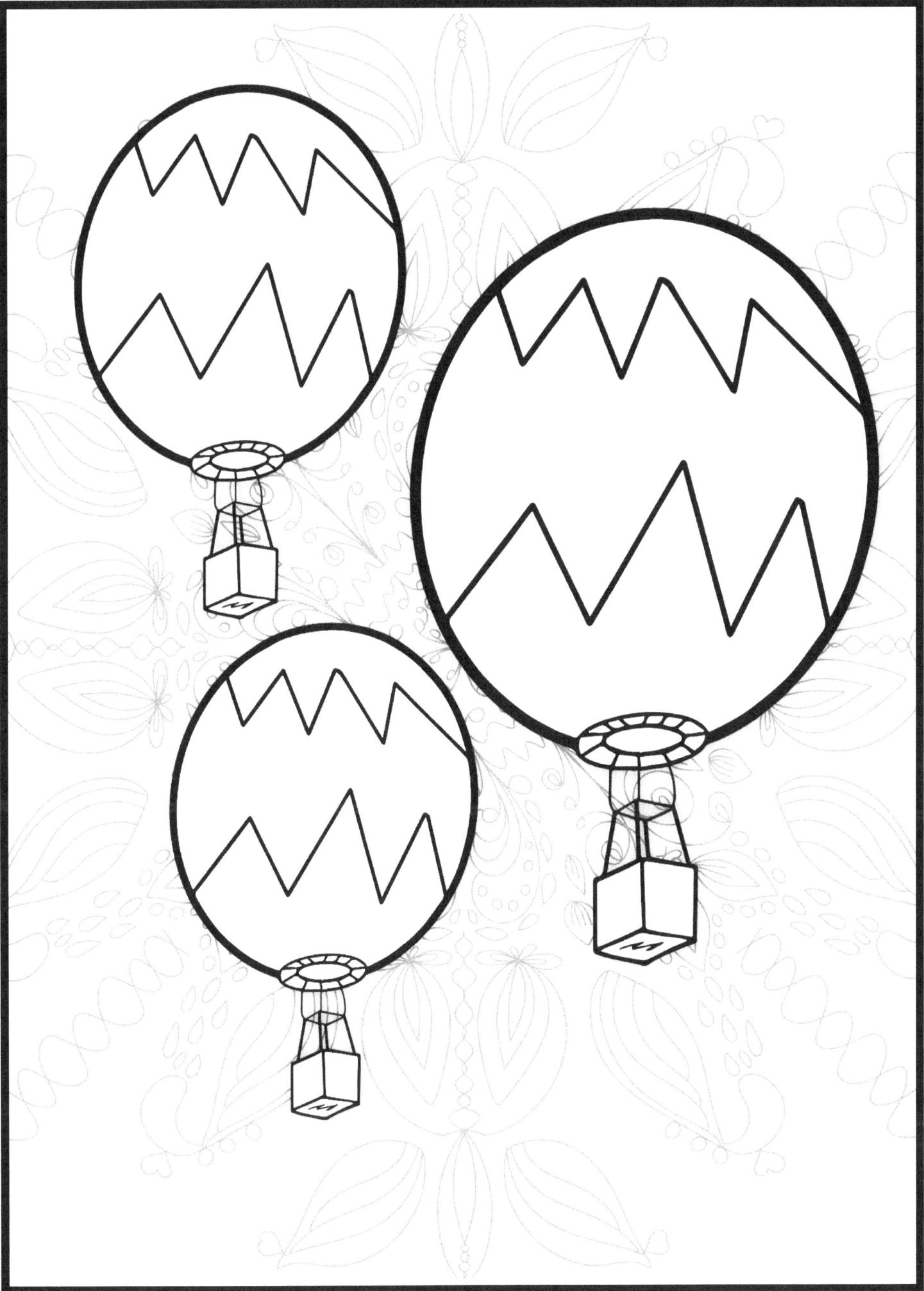

Up and Away

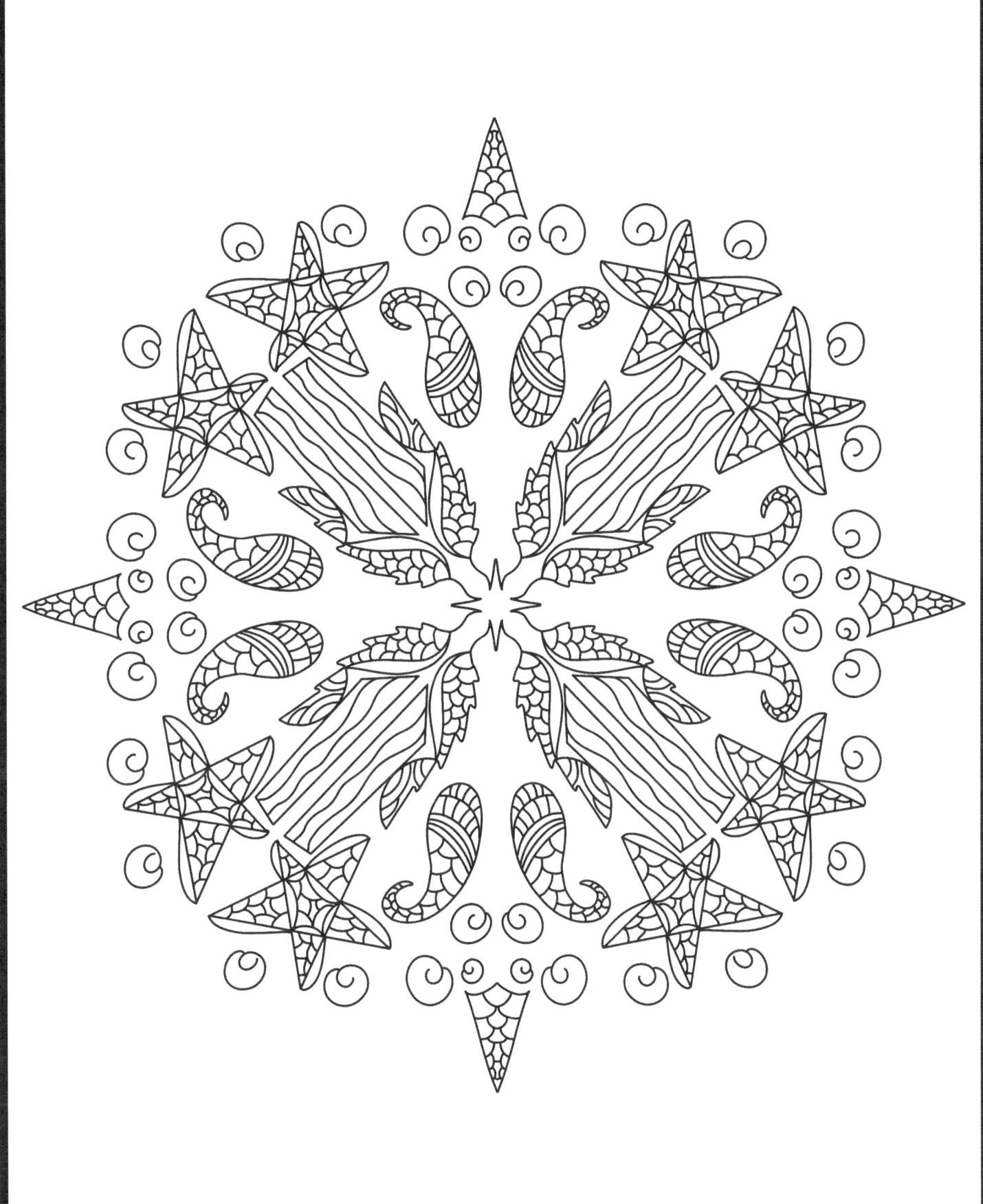

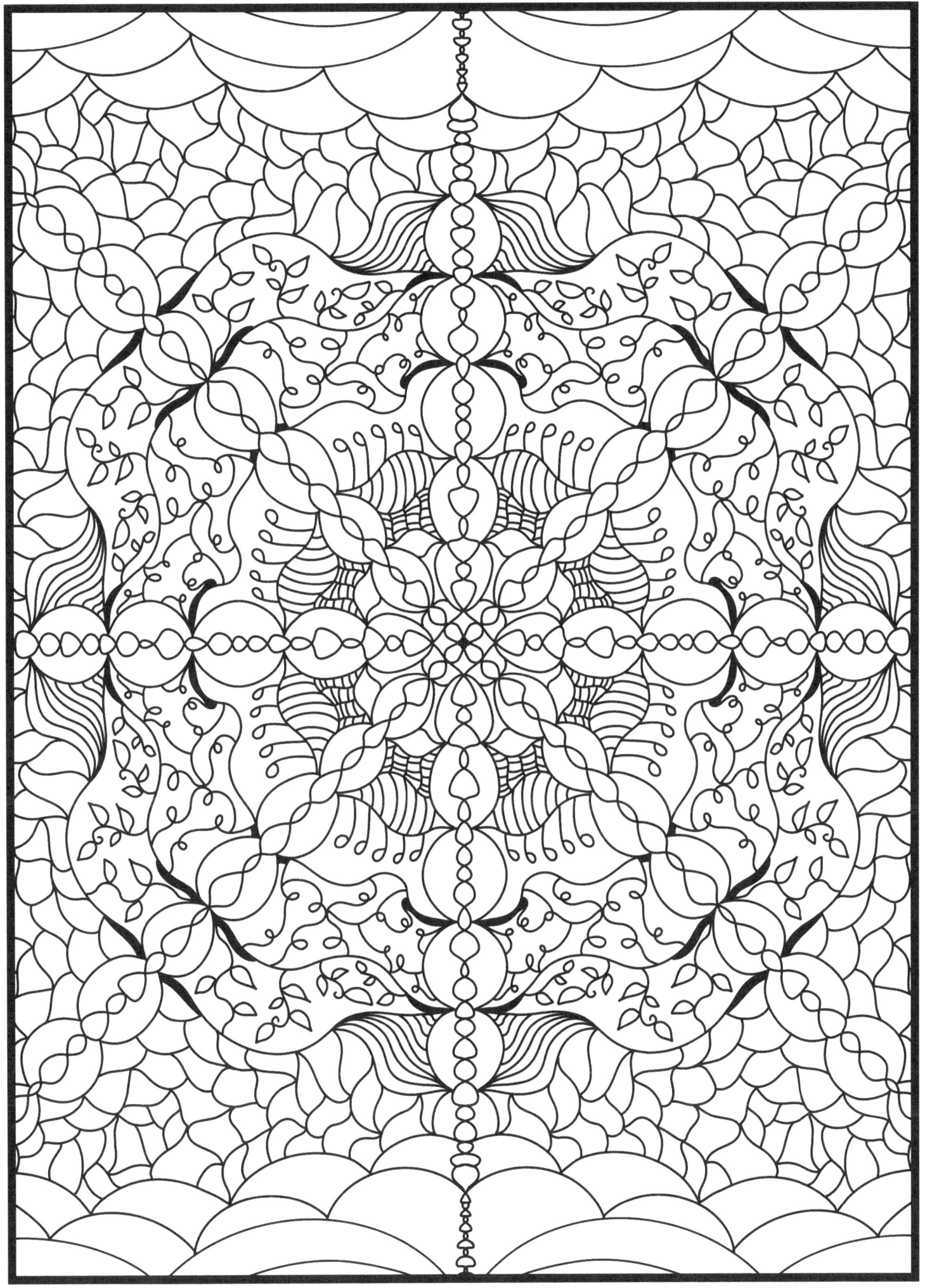

Florets

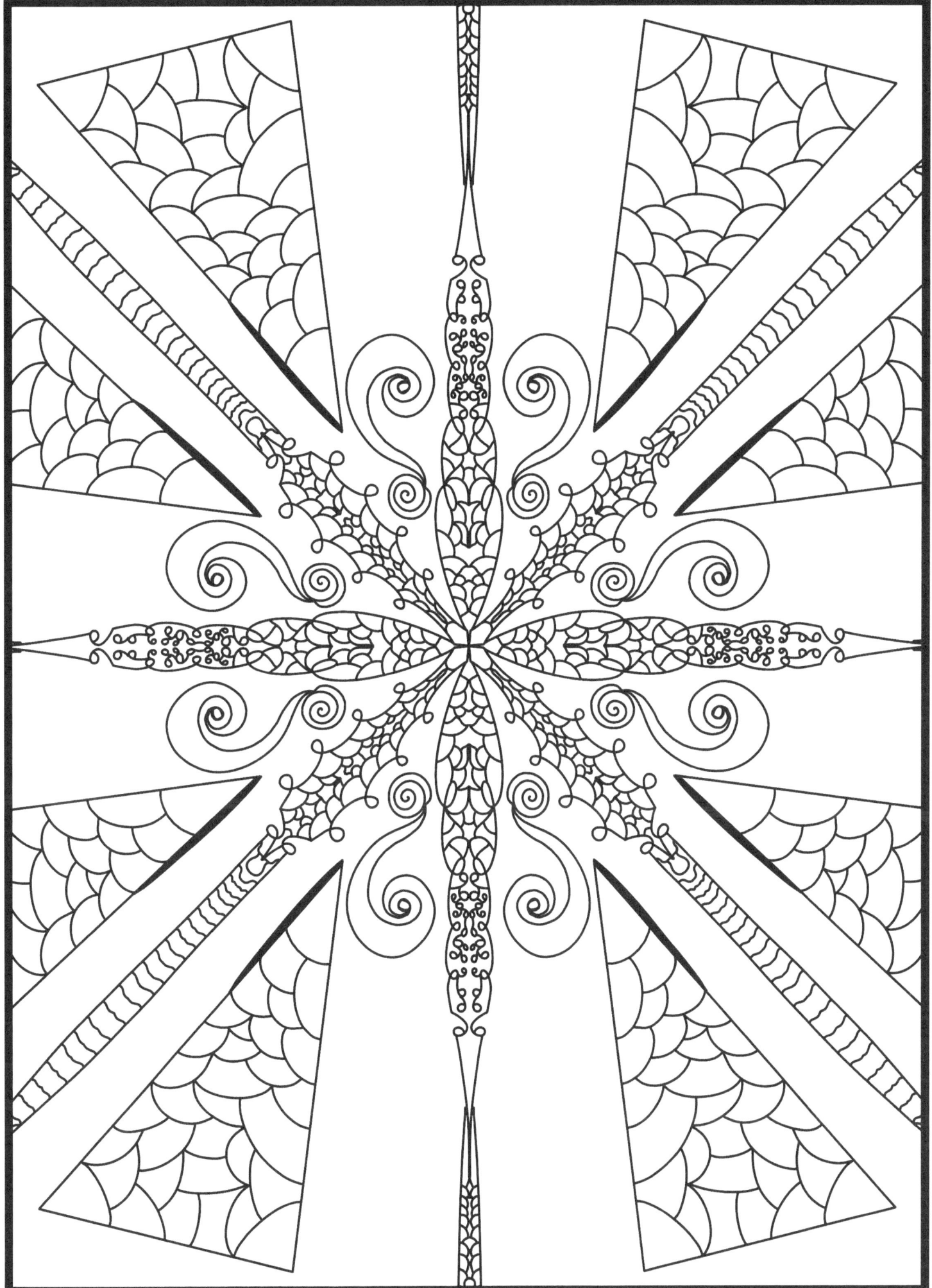

Snow Crystals

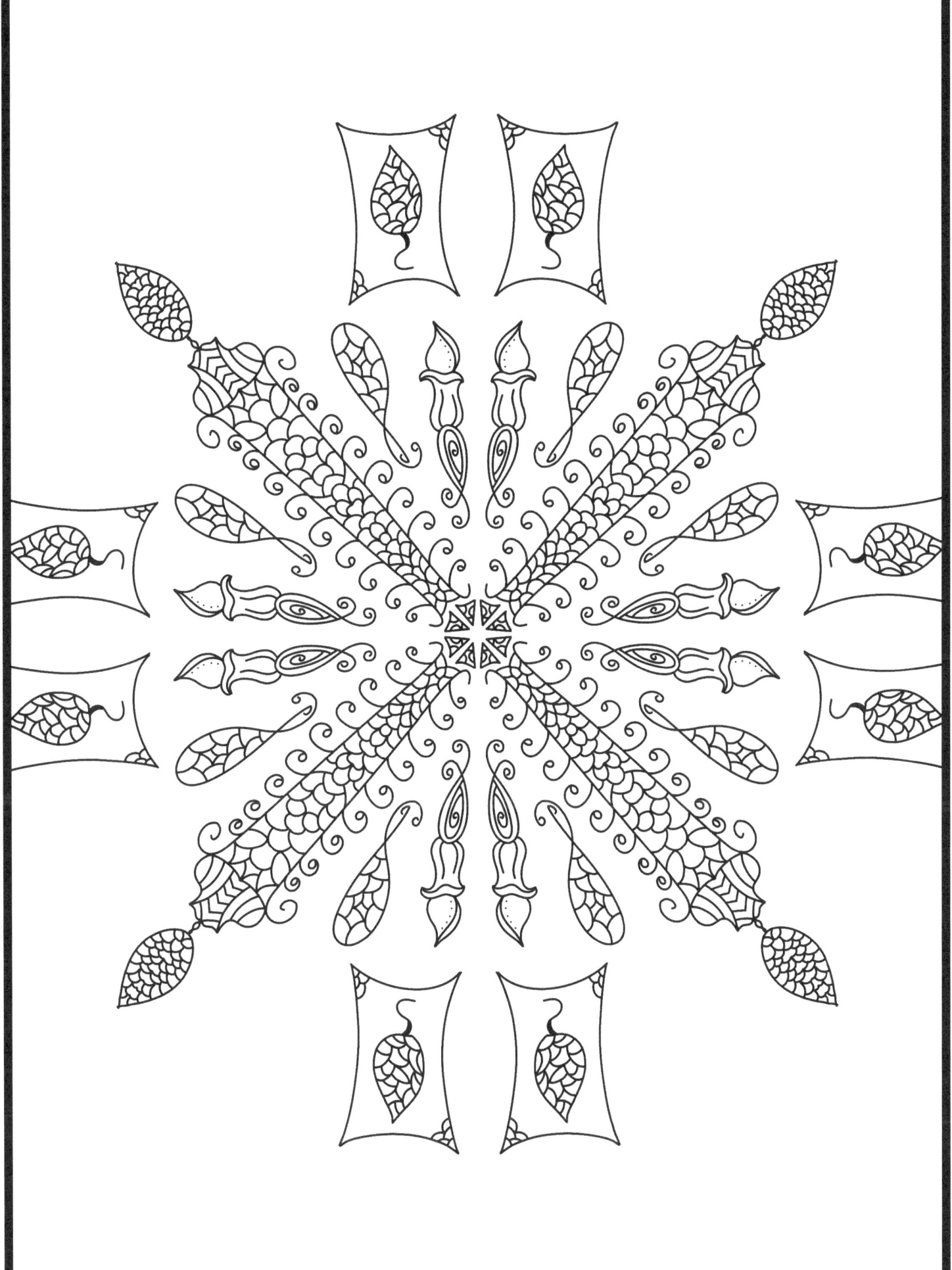

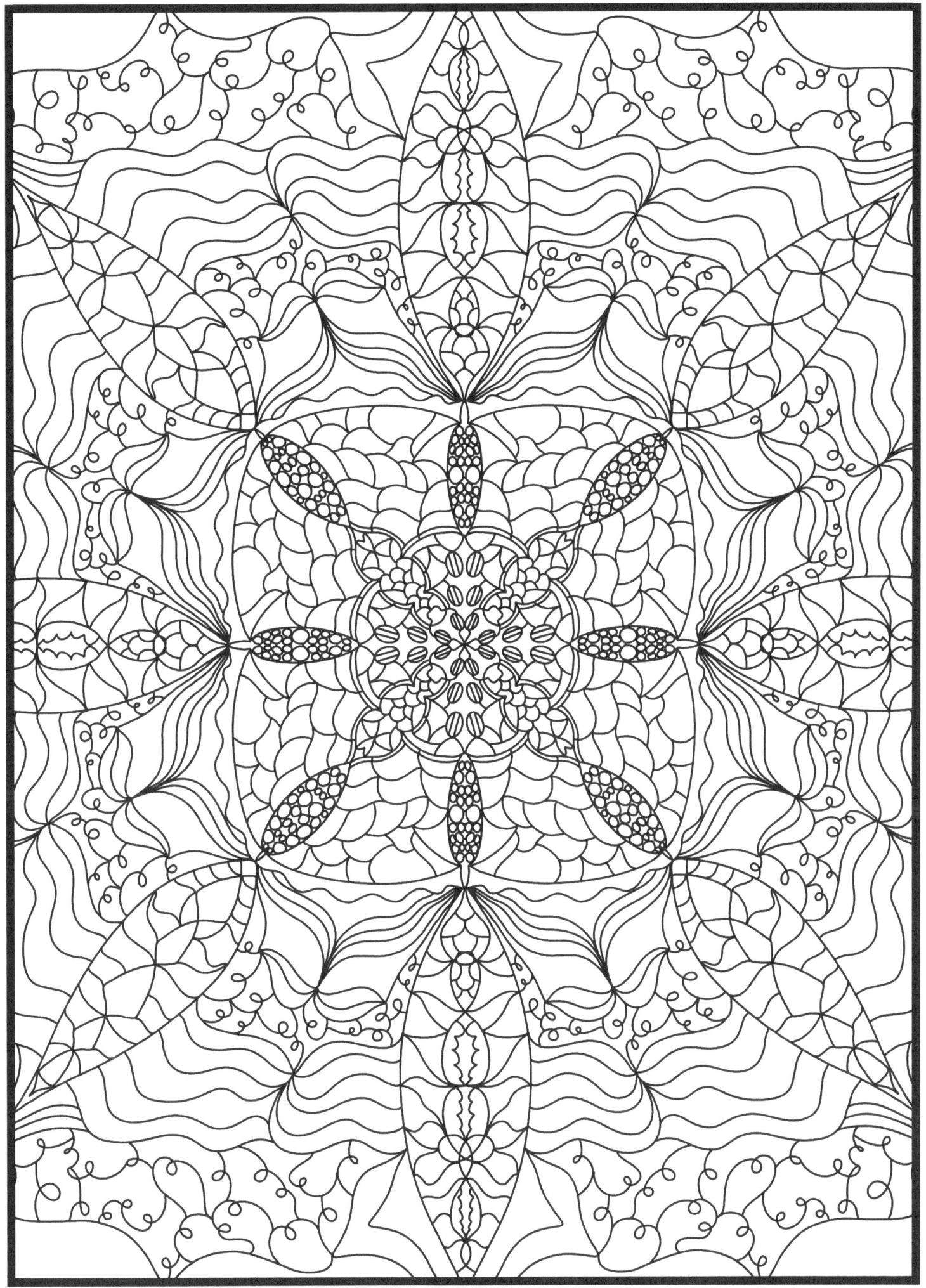

Stain Glass Window

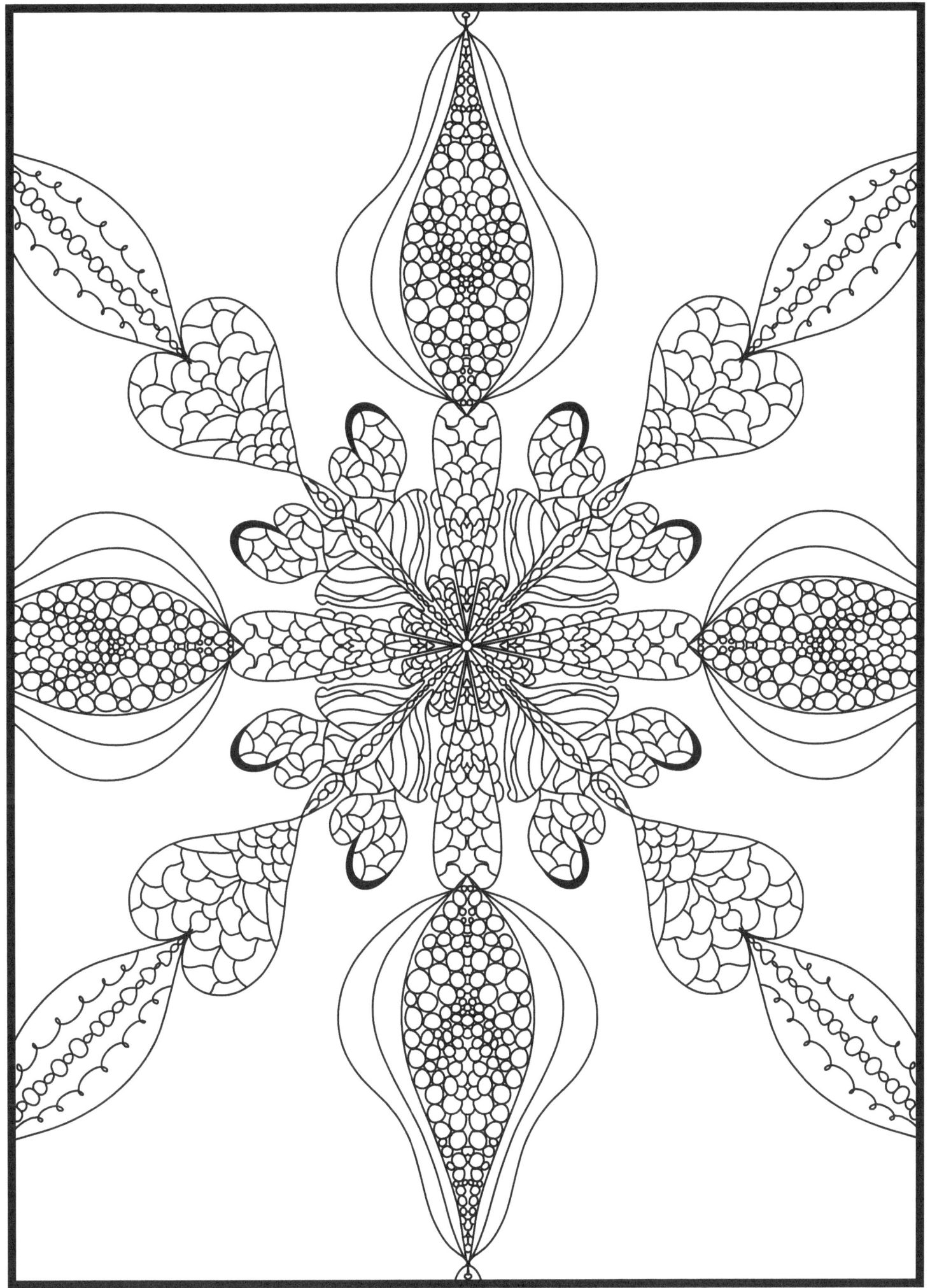

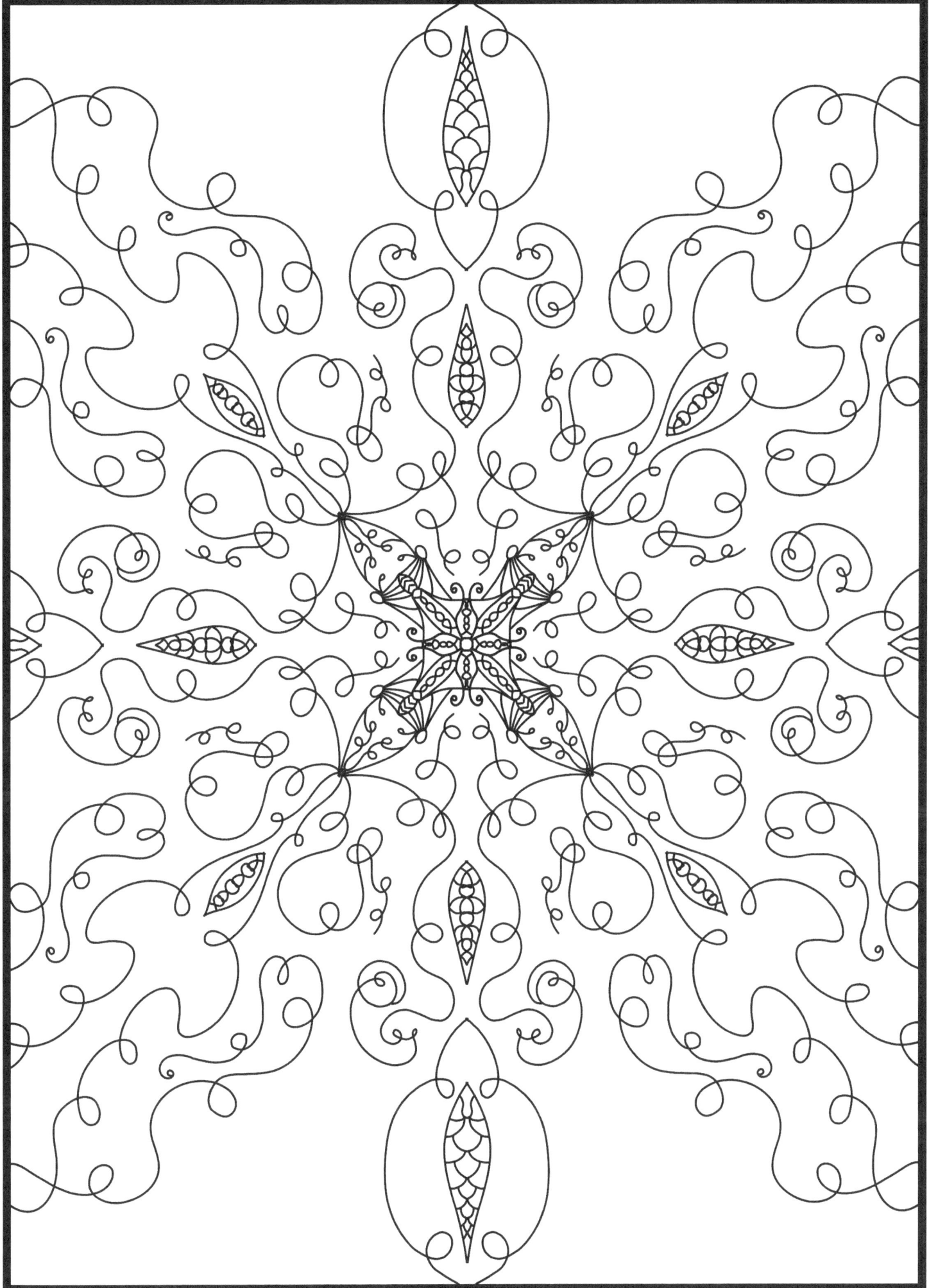

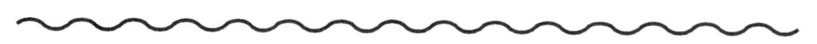

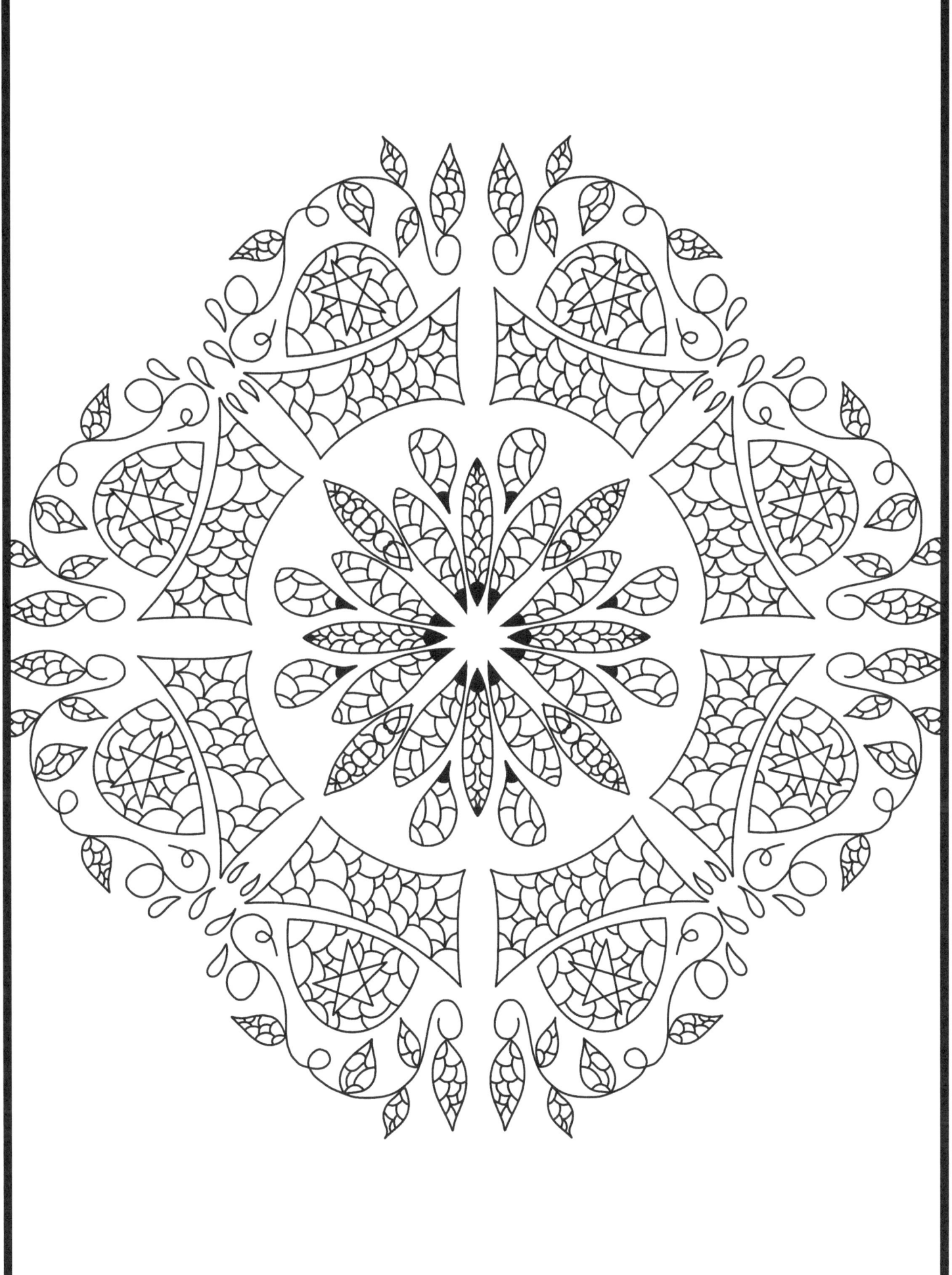

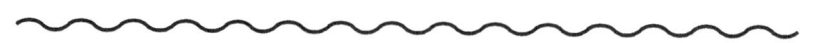

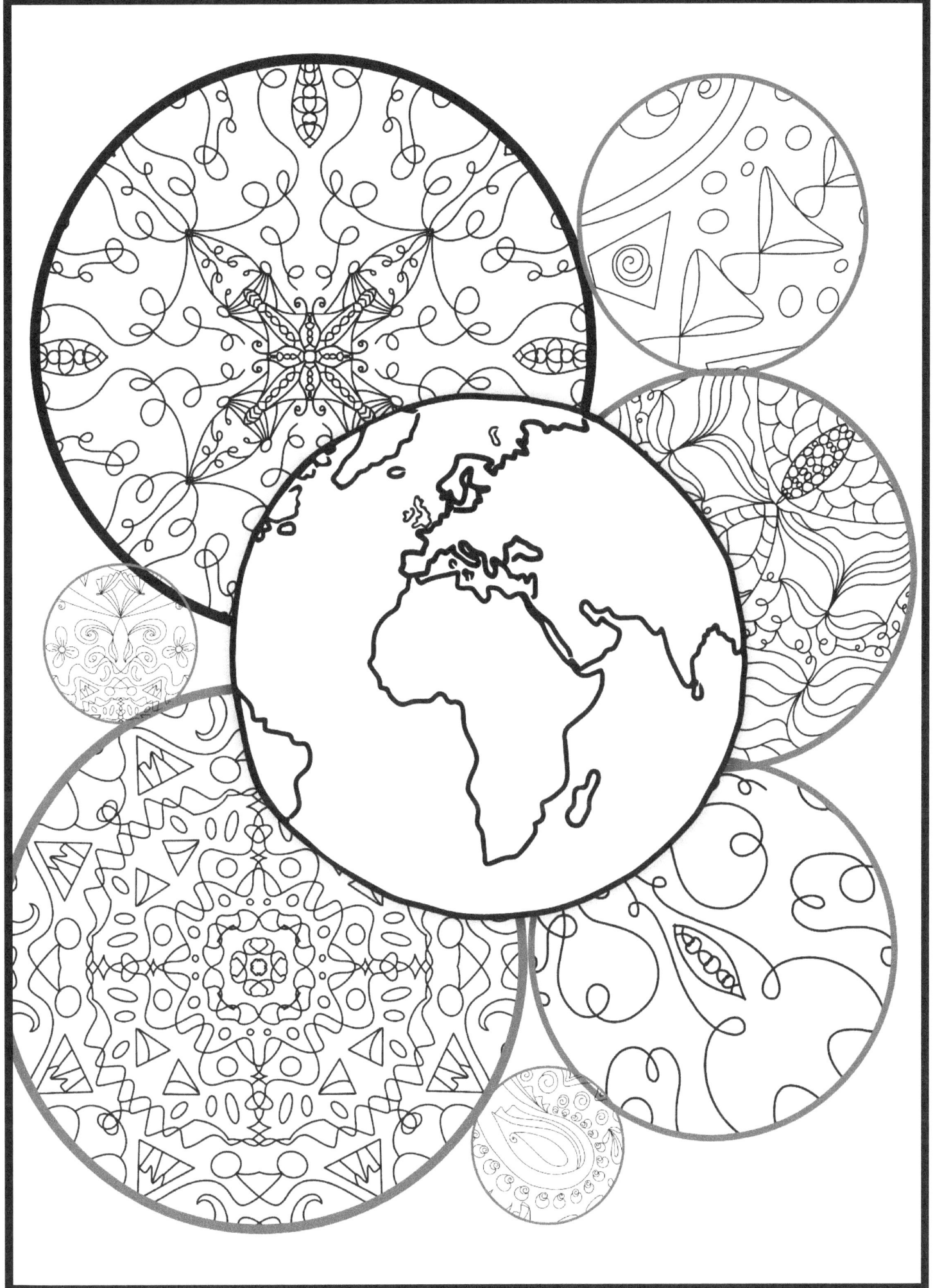

Earth

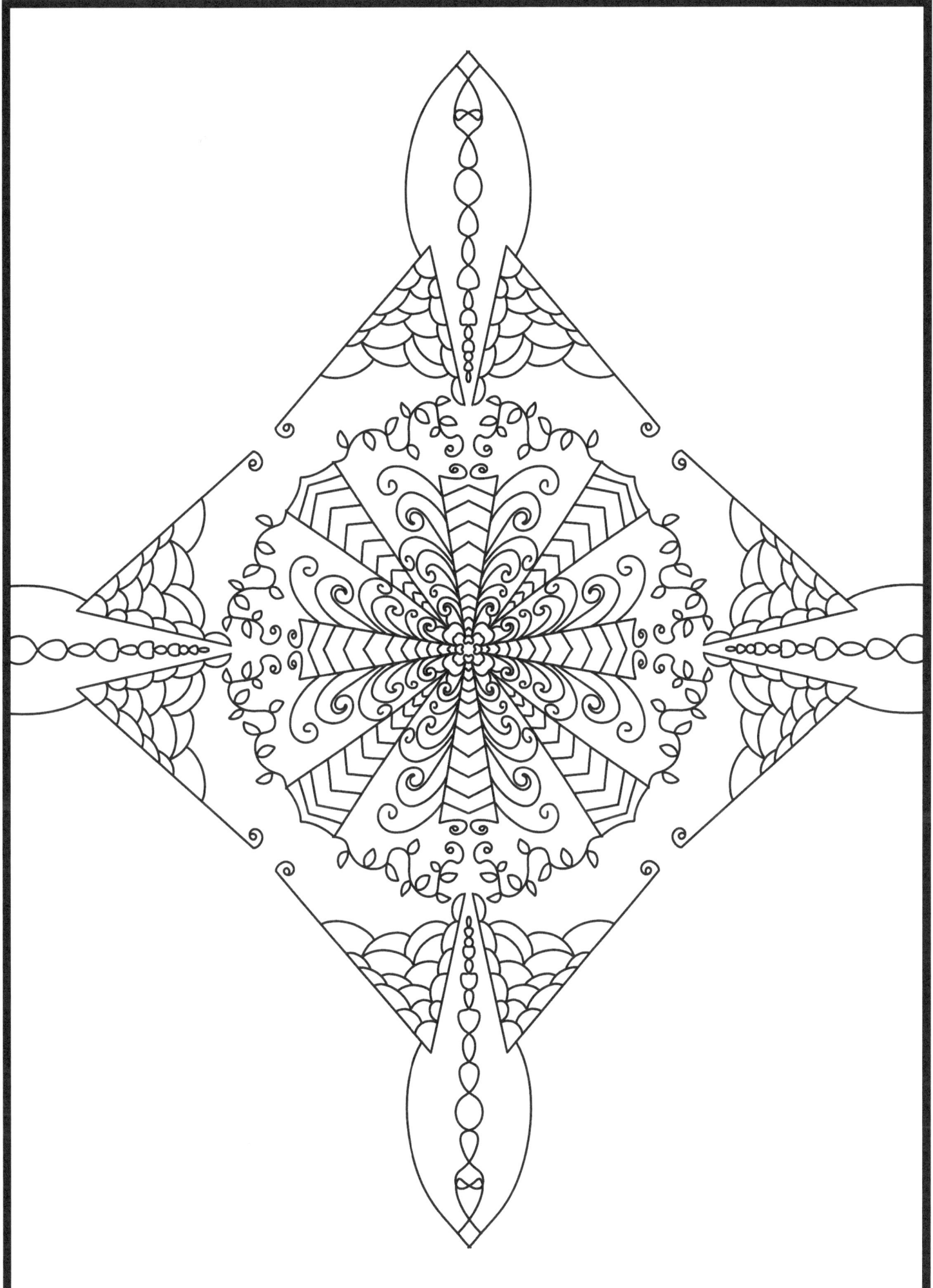

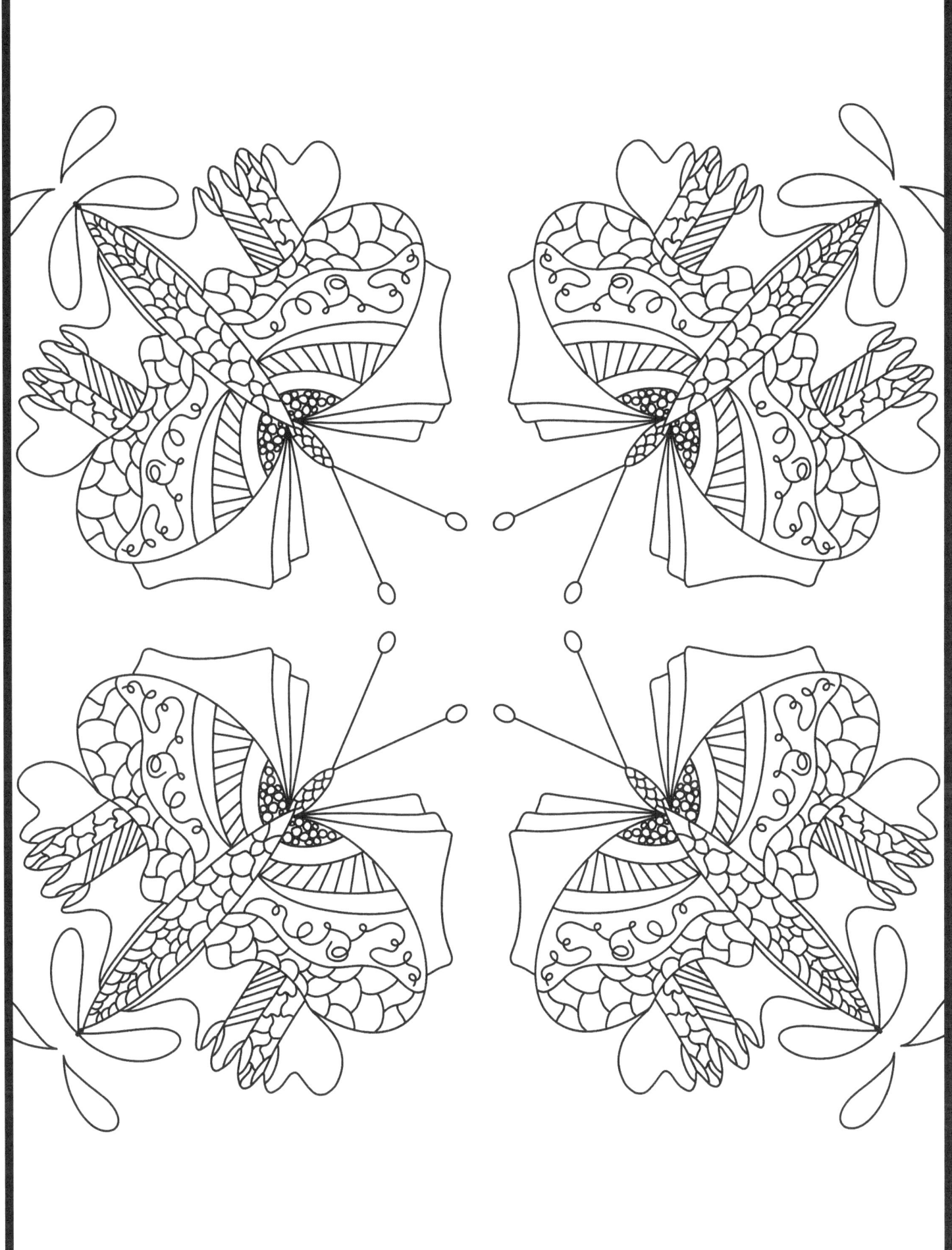

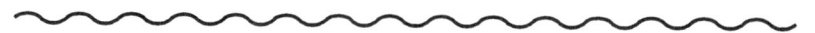

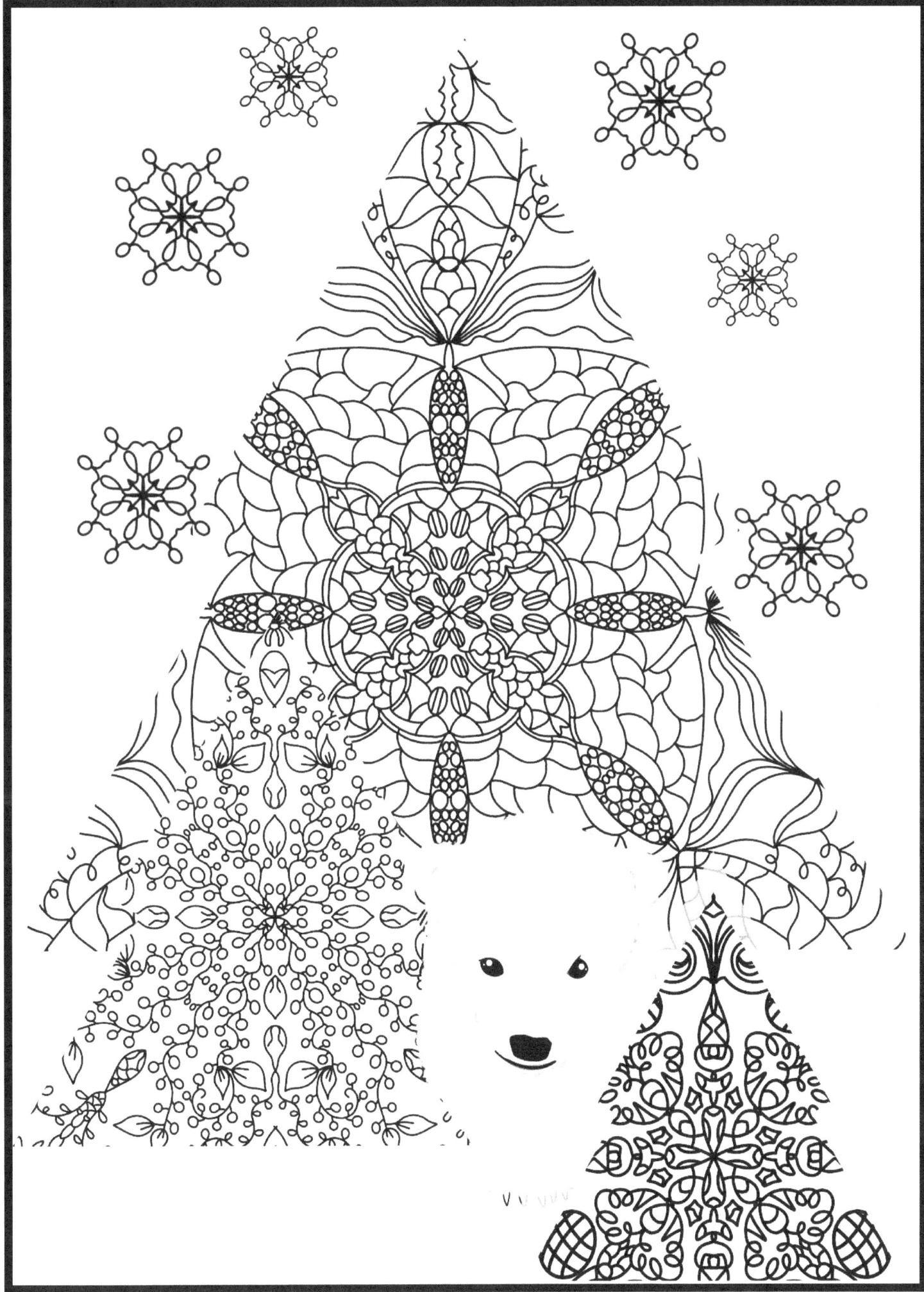

North Pole

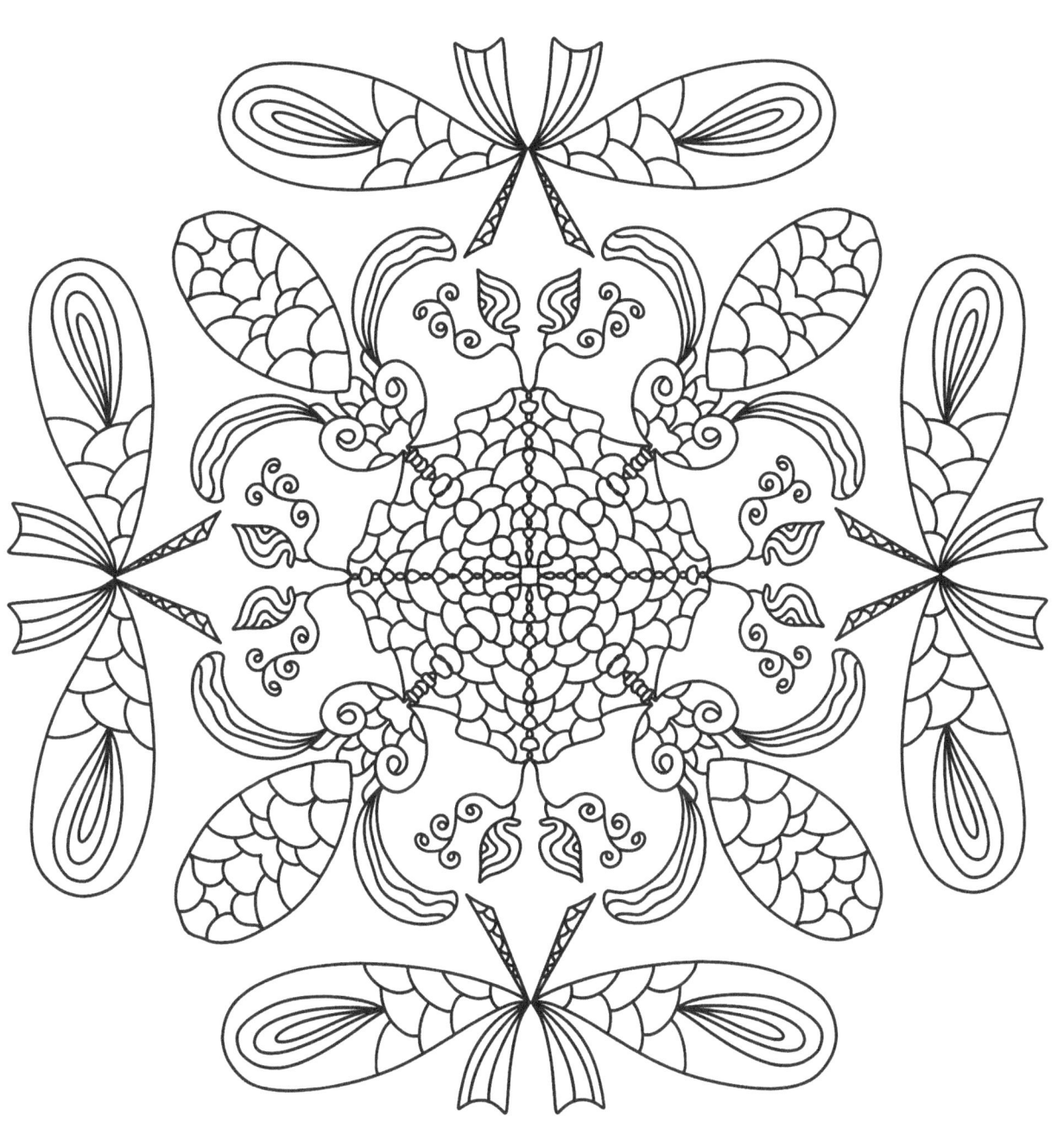

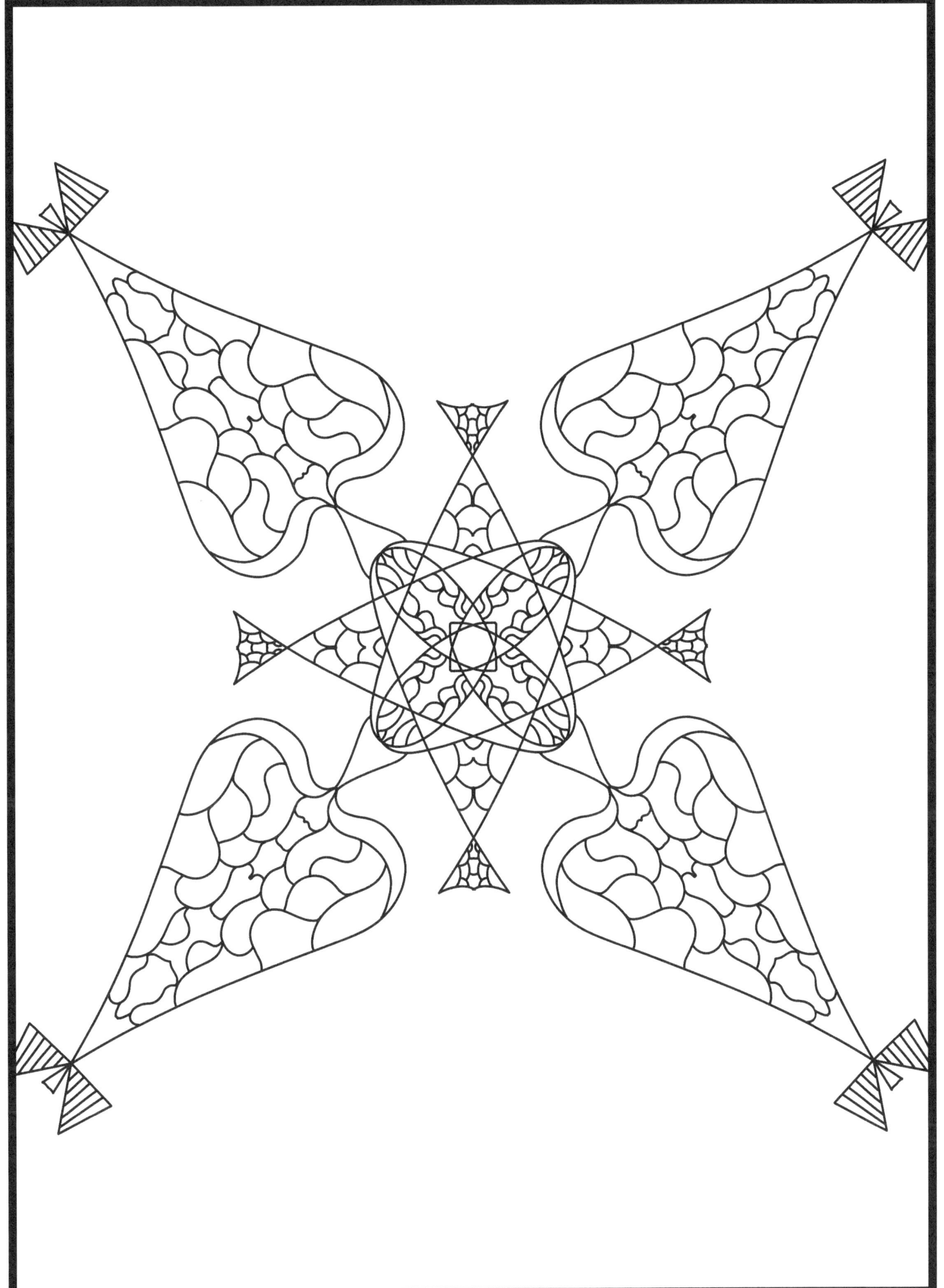

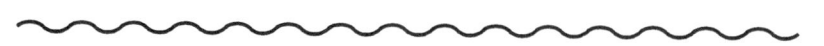

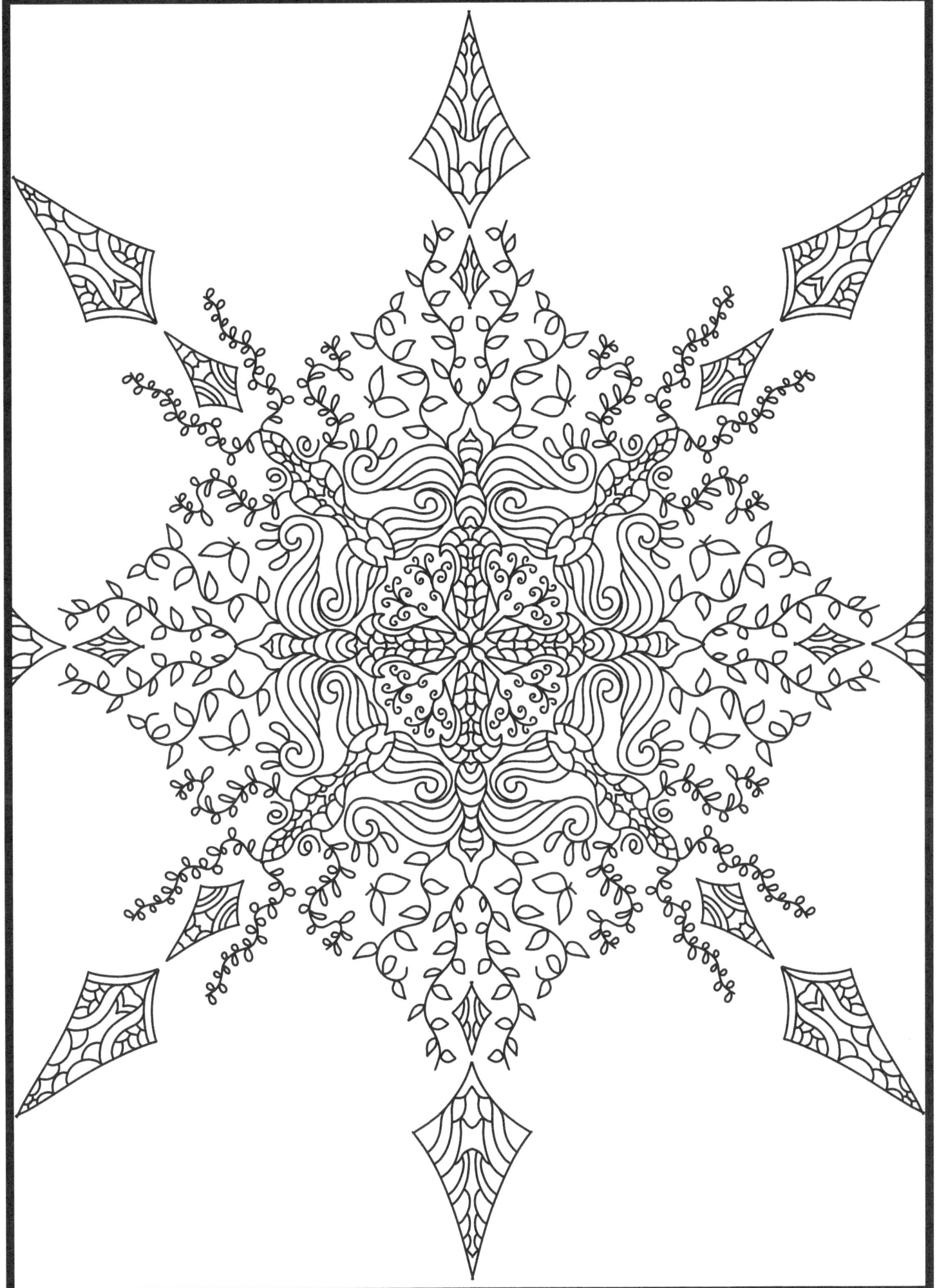

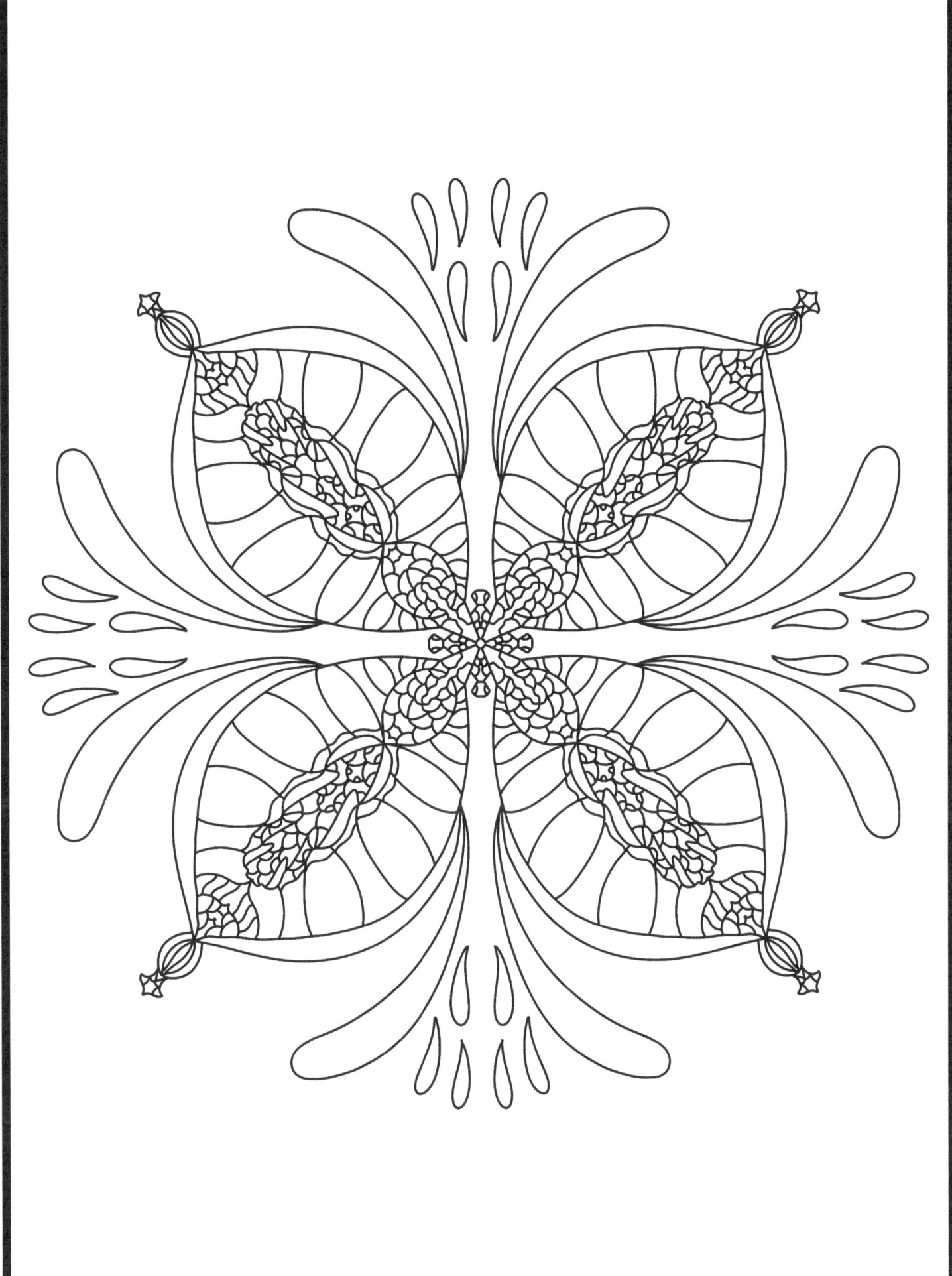

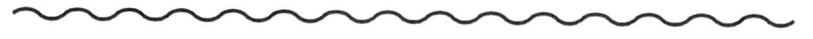

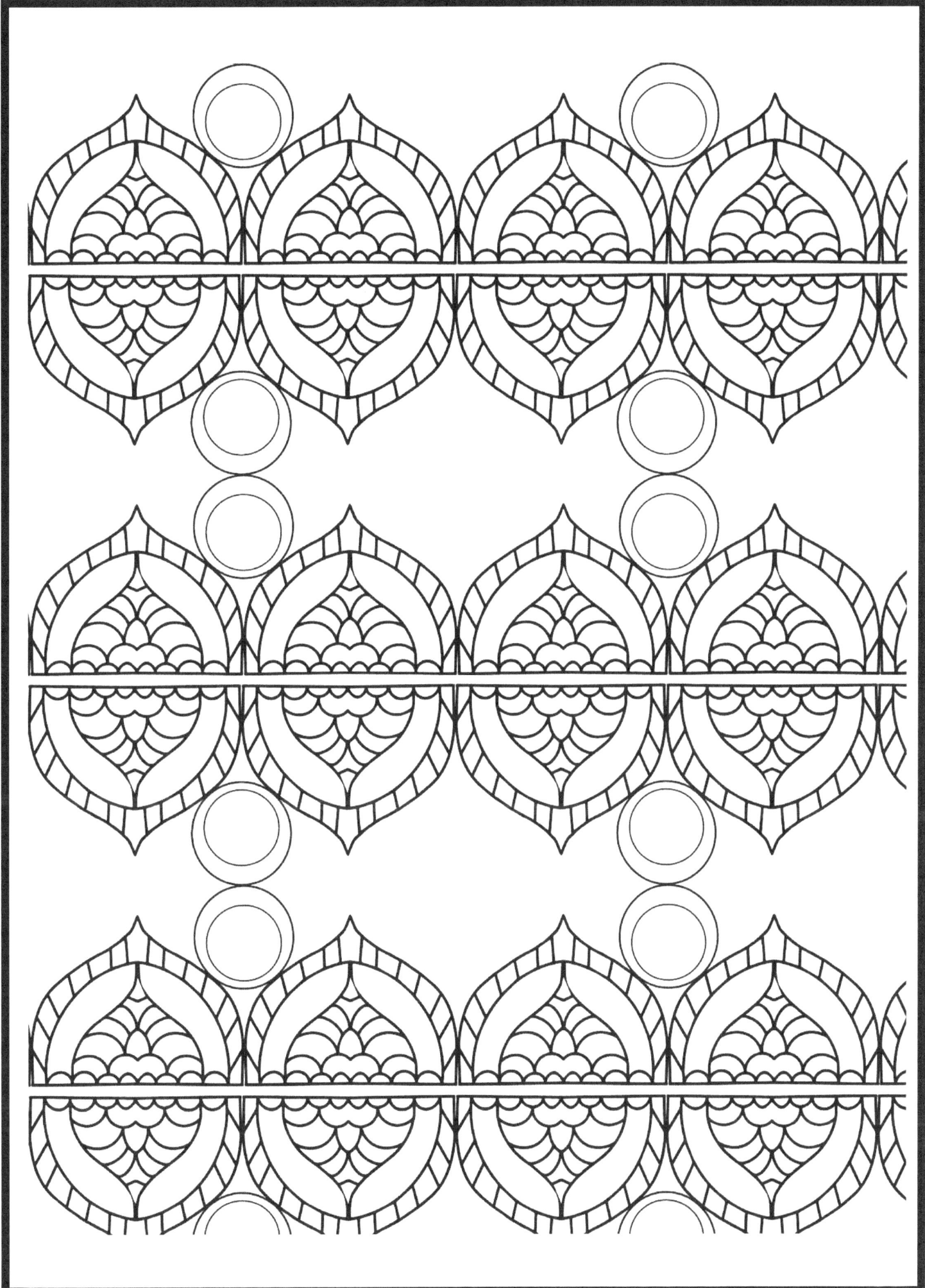

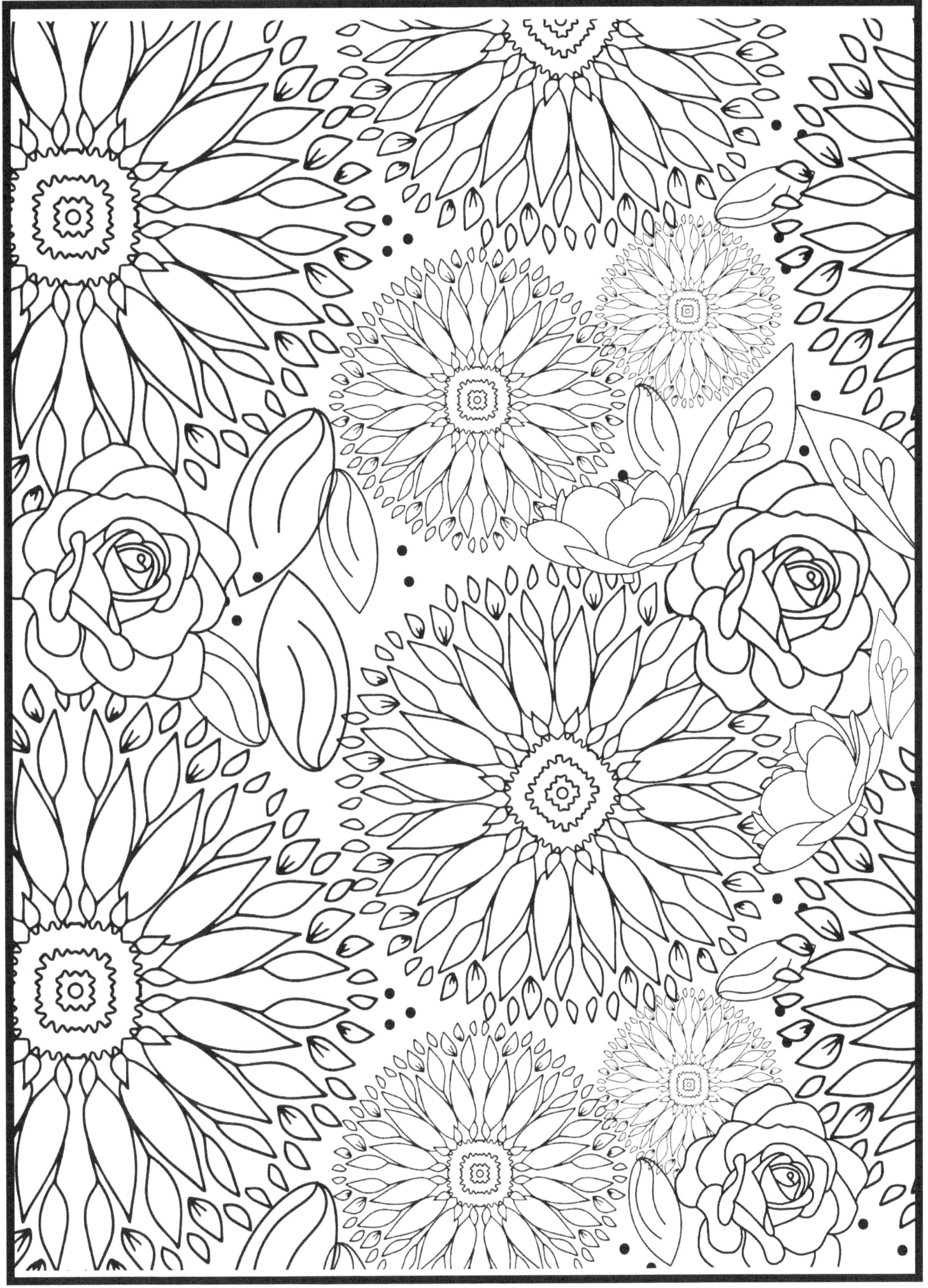

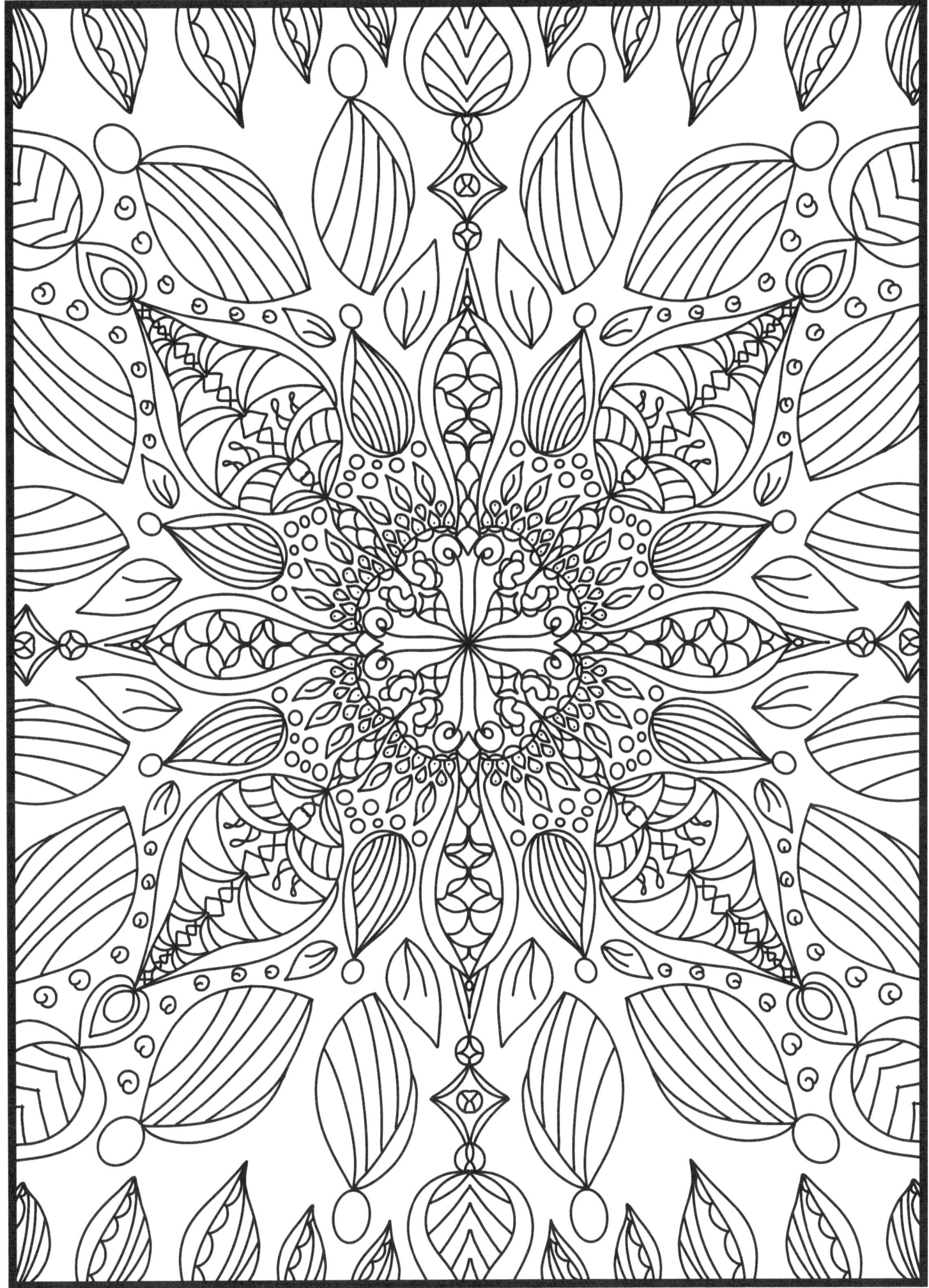

Forest Leaves

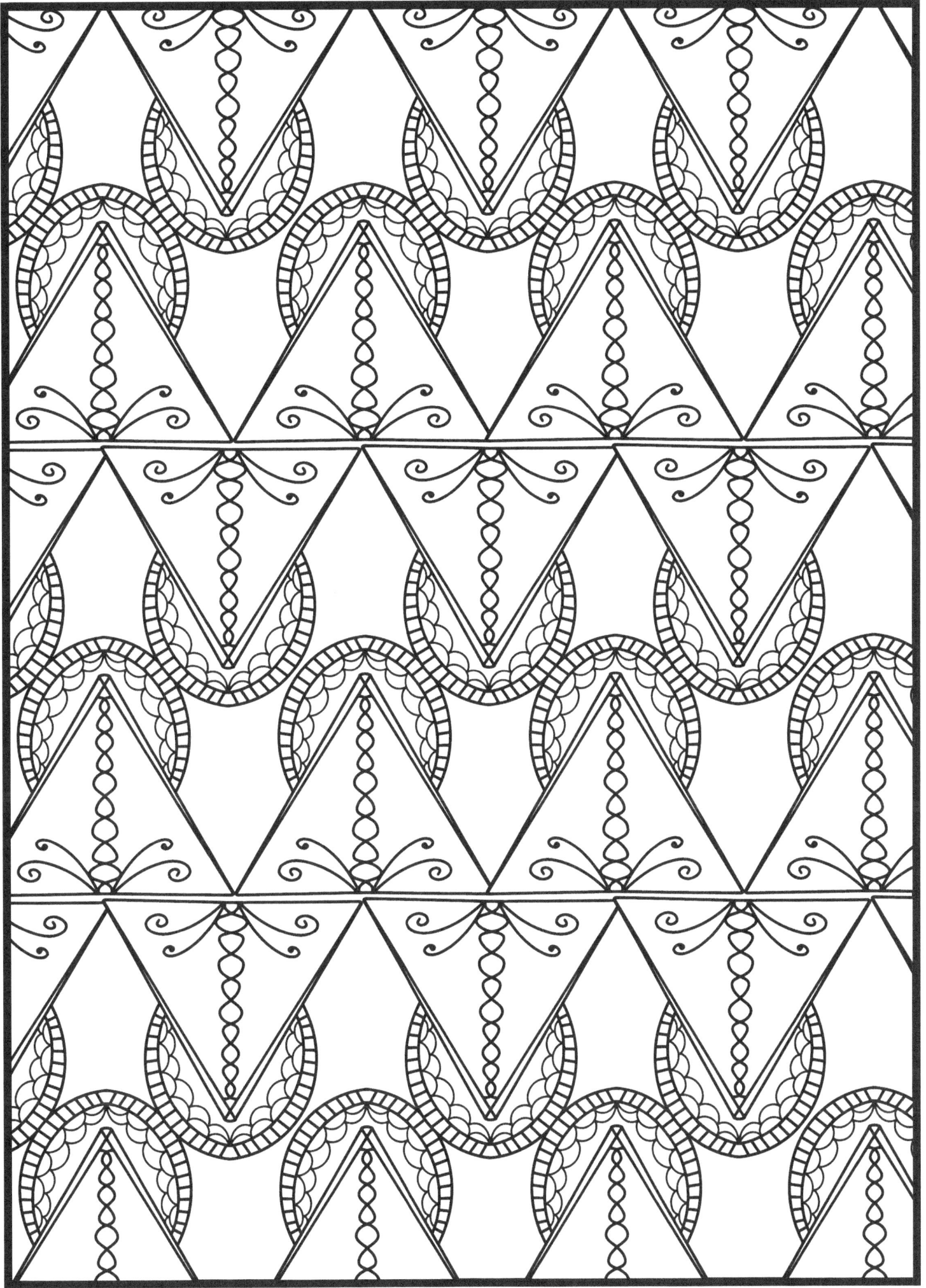

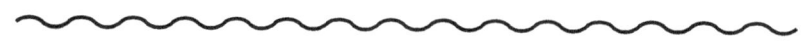

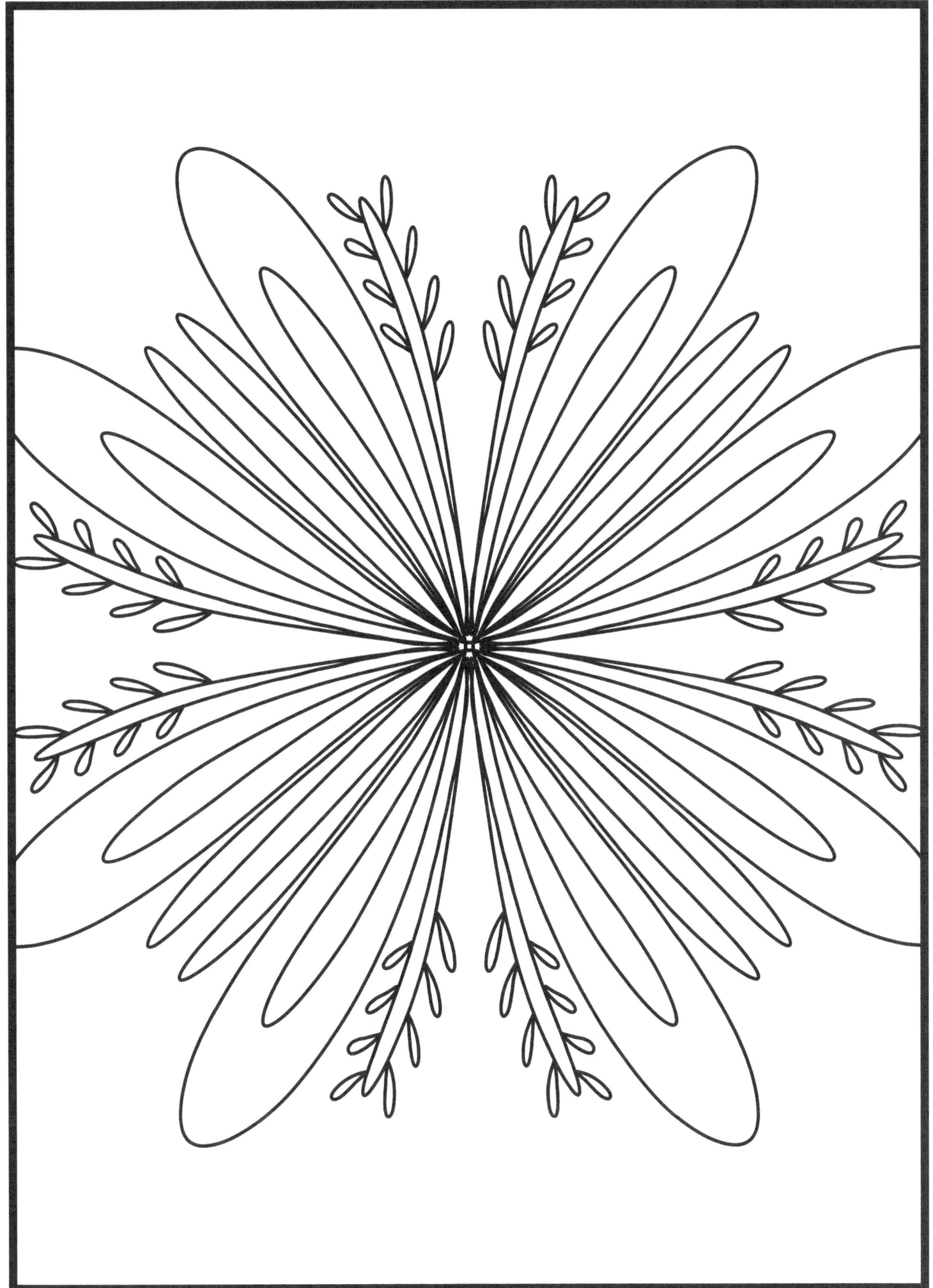

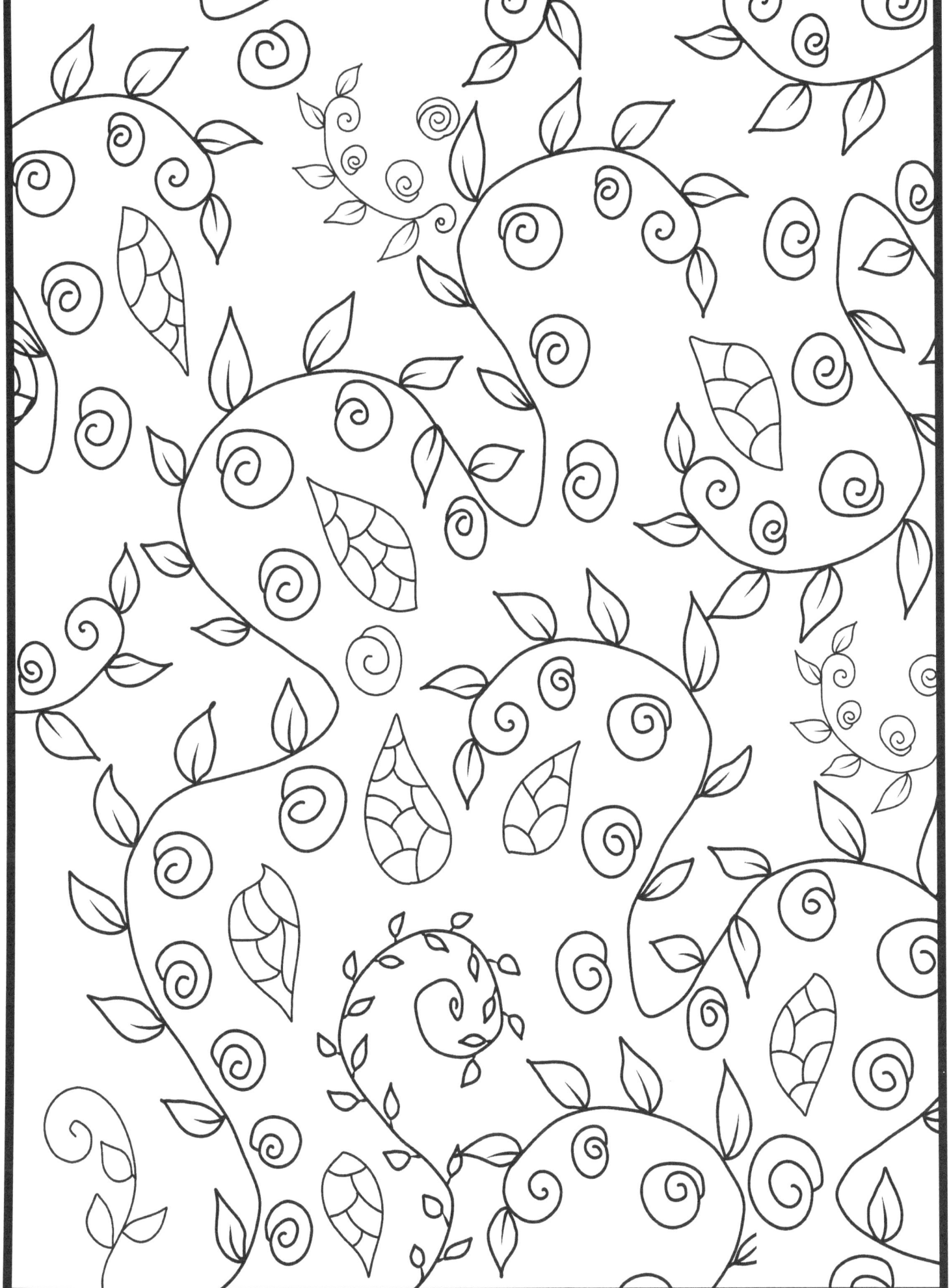

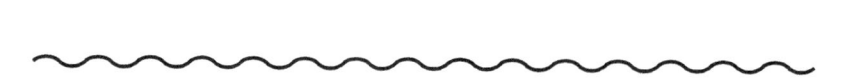

www.ingramcontent.com/pod-product-compliance
Lightning Source LLC
Chambersburg PA
CBHW080455220526
45465CB00006B/2277